Got to Live

923 Days to Remember

Jay Danek

First edition

ISBN-13: 978-1489587602
ISBN-10: 1489587608

Editor: Susan Fish/Storywell
http://storywell.ca/

Book design: Y42K Book Production Services
http://www.y42k.com/bookproduction.html

Cover design: John Vaupel
http://www.johnvaupel.com/

Cover photo: Glenn Tachiyama
http://www.tachifoto.net/

Contents

Dedication

This book is dedicated to my parents, who meant everything to me when I was growing up. My parents have been the most influential people in my life and they are two people who would do anything for anybody without ever thinking about themselves.

My father T never wanted anything from life except for his family to be happy and to teach others patience, kindness, and why family is so important. While T will never get to see my daughter Petra grow up, I am blessed that he was around for her early in life and even though she was 8 1/2 months old last time she saw him, she points him out in pictures every day and says "I love you and miss you, Papa." He is a presence in my life that I know is watching over us all the day and just a look up to him gets me through any difficult moment. I miss you every day, T, and not a day goes by that we don't talk on the mountain summit.

While my mom lives 2,000 miles away, she continues to carry on my dad's legacy and she has been very instrumental in helping me achieve my goals in life from school to work to running. I talk to my mom often and I know my dad would be proud of how she has carried on and continues to be a huge influence in my family's life. Losing your husband of 36 years is one of the most difficult things a spouse can go through, but my mom has learned to celebrate her husband's life, and her positive nature as a parent never skipped a beat.

Thank you for everything you two have done for me in making me the person I am today.

Foreword

Life is full of challenges. We all get knocked down and our response to that adversity defines our lives. For many veterans of the Iraq and Afghanistan wars, that "knock down moment" often comes when they lose someone close to them. And while our country's service members have dealt with this a lot over the past decade, it's actually common ground that they share with anyone who has lost someone close to them---common ground with great Americans like Jay Danek.

I have only met Jay in person once. It was Veterans Day weekend 2012 in the hill country of Texas, at a place called Camp Eagle. I was there to represent Team Red, White & Blue in a three-day trail running training camp. Jay and I arrived in the parking lot at the same time; he was there to serve as a mentor and coach. It was a hectic few days, filled with a lot of running, learning and camaraderie. Because of this, I didn't get to spend much time with Jay but I knew a little bit about his recent history---and would come to know a lot more about his journey in the coming months.

Like anyone, I was fascinated by Jay's shift from non-runner to ultra-marathoner---and how rapidly and effectively he made this transition. However, as a student of positive psychology, I was even more inspired by Jay's perseverance and resilience. That is the most critical part of this remarkable story from which we can all draw inspiration.

As the Founder and Chairman of the Board for Team Red, White & Blue, I have interacted with hundreds of military veterans who have lost fellow service members under their command, serving to their right and left. Whether it's a fellow soldier, best friend, sister or father, loss is painful. I am reminded of this every single day as a leader in Team RWB. And while it is very easy to allow loss to drive you down the path of darkness---as Jay knows all too well and recounts in this book---it is also possible to battle those demons and beat them into submission. That is the moral of Jay Danek's remarkable story.

So how did Jay pull out of his downward spiral? Family, exercise and purpose. Jay is fortunate to have a patient and supportive family. That is the first building block and one that Jay discusses in depth in this book. Exercise is a powerful weapon and scientifically proven to be as effective at battling depression as medication is---with fewer side effects. Once Jay uncovered the power of exercise, he started to take heavy doses of it. Doses that would make the average runner's jaw drop. Dose after dose. As you read running stories that are inspiring, entertaining and remarkable, you can almost feel yourself recovering alongside Jay as he narrates his journey and grows stronger with each mile.

Family and exercise are two-thirds of the equation, but that wasn't the full story that allowed Jay to make a complete recovery from the loss of his father and his subsequent depression. It's only complete when you talk about purpose. I believe in the power of relentlessly pursuing our purpose in life. Jay's story calls to mind a powerful comment that award-winning actor Will Smith made on the subject of loss:

> "I've been really intrigued by the human response to emotional trauma, and that exploration has yielded epiphany after epiphany for me. We all are going to experience death, and not just literal, physical death; figurative death. We're going to lose our jobs; we're going to lose loved ones. Why do some people get depressed and shut down and disconnect, and some people find the energy to rumble and become Nelson Mandela?"
>
> "When you can connect your life to a purpose, to an idea beyond yourself, it becomes bigger than your loss, bigger than your pain. It almost becomes this fantastic spiritual ladder that you climb out of your emotional hole."

For seven months after the death of his father, Jay wandered without an understanding of his purpose, but then he found it. And little bit by little bit, that sense of purpose grew. Jay describes how badly he struggled in a "fitness boot camp" early in his recovery; his purpose started with not wanting his daughter to see him fail. It didn't take long before that purpose rapidly grew into becoming an example for other people---showing them that no matter how difficult the struggles are or how long they last, we can regain control over our lives. In writing this book, where Jay opens himself up to anyone who reads Got to Live, he has taken his sense of purpose to a new level. His story is one of hope and it will inspire anyone who reads it---but most importantly, it will encourage people who are in a dark place who need a reminder that they can regain control over their life, just like Jay.

-Mike Erwin, President of Team Red, White, and Blue

Introduction

As a child, I never understood how others could wait patiently until Christmas morning to see which gifts awaited them under the tree. From the minute the first shiny packages showed up, I would anxiously shake each one to determine what was inside. I would ruin birthday surprises because I would snoop around the house days before my birthday until I found what my mom and dad had bought for me. As an adult, this impatience translated into my inability to slow down enough to be truly present in any one situation. I found myself constantly thinking of what was next and it prevented me from enjoying myself until I could find out.

It took one early-morning phone call in the fall of 2008 for me to change my way of thinking; to see life in a new way. This is the story of how that phone call and the events that followed it both completely stopped and also resurrected my life.

Chapter 1: Zane Grey 50-Miler

First, let's fast forward to April 16, 2011. Sitting in my car on this cold April morning I began to wonder what the day had in store for me. The Zane Grey 50-Mile Endurance Run travels from Pine, Ariz., to Christopher Creek along the historic Highline Trail. Runner friends talked about it being the hardest 50-mile race in the country and others warned me about the difficult navigation out on the course. Never being great with maps, I went into the race expecting to get lost and hoping to prove myself wrong. To add to my fear, I scanned the website instructions, which reminded runners that the race was extremely difficult. Race directors asked those who were not used to the 50- to 100- mile distances to shy away and come back when they had more experience. I did neither, and with only one 50-mile run under my belt, I toed the line of yet another ultra-event.

At this point I told myself, "You are here, might as well turn on your headlight, shake out your arms and legs and prepare for a long and grueling day." One hundred twenty-four of us crazies stood around the starting line pretending that the 40-degree weather did not bother us. My mind wandered to the stories friends had etched into my mind for the past six months. Treacherous rocks, burn areas, wildlife, scenery, difficult terrain—in my mind there was no way it would live up to the hype.

Of the runners I stood amongst at the starting line, the field boasted several elite ultra-runners from across the country, one from as far away as Alaska. They had traveled a long distance to run this race and without question were there to put on a show and to compete.

The average finish time at Zane Grey hovers around 13.5 hours. I went into the race with a goal of finishing in 12–12.5 hours. Whether I would be running, shuffling or just walking, I knew this was going to be a long day on my feet. We took off and headed through the dark woods, making our way to the first moderate climb of the day. Slowly but surely the field of runners began to separate. Soon gaps opened up on the single track trail that wound through the mountains. Because it was dark, I couldn't see much during the first part of the race. This reminded me of the importance of careful footing over speed. Of course, this was much easier said than done when running over rocks, up hills, and through narrow, eroded trenches. I ran along at a decent pace for the first four miles and then as the sun started to rise I suddenly felt like it was time to open up the legs a little and push the pace. Being the inexperienced runner I was, I can now laugh at the fact that I decided to "push it" at mile four of 50.

The next uphill granted me the opportunity to make a nice cushion between runners. I should have reminded myself to take this cushion with a grain of salt. No sooner was I feeling the endorphins of passing others, when a root grabbed hold of my ankles and threw me to the ground. This wasn't just any fall; it was like a slow-motion sack of a quarterback. It wasn't one of those falls that you can fight off by waving your arms real fast with Superman form to keep from falling. Instead it was a slow, ugly fall, right into the wet leaves littering the ground. Not only did I go down but I nearly took out the runner in front of me as I somersaulted and hit the ground hard, face first. I brushed myself off, picked my broken Garmin watch-band up off the ground, found my iPod, and wiped the mud off my face before finally getting myself back on the trail. I might have gone 500 yards before the same thing happened to me again! This time I was able to laugh it off and realize I really should be looking out for the buried roots instead of only the big rocks I was fumbling around on.

Rolling into mile six, I felt I now had a firm grasp of the course and had finally figured out how to maneuver the roots, but when I slowed down around a tight corner, my feet immediately locked up again in some roots and down I went. This time I cut my left knee open on a rock and was flustered. How can one person trip and fall three times in the first six miles of a 50-mile race? At this point I began to have doubts about the day and thought maybe this course just wasn't for me. I was quickly losing my ability to brush off another fall. Were the horror stories I had heard from my friends about the difficulty of this course true? Would I be able to handle a whole day of this? I kept telling myself to shake it off and move on.

Just as I began to remove the negative thoughts from my mind, I found myself lying on the ground again, picking dirt out of my teeth.

I got up, this time uttering a profanity or two, and then immediately tripped again.

Up, down. Up, down. Up, down, down, down.

Five falls before the first aid station. I was still ahead of schedule, but banged up, embarrassed, and flustered. Running hard into the Geronimo aid station, I filled my backpack, got my head together and headed out. I wanted to laugh, cry, and most of all quit. But at this point I realized that the more I stressed over the situation, the worse it was going to be for me and I moved forward. Since no crews were allowed at this station, it afforded me the opportunity to make a quick stop and I looked forward to seeing familiar faces at mile 17.

Running through the woods, I laughed with a few friends about my fancy footwork. Time and miles seemed irrelevant as I relayed the stories of my stupidity in the previous section. The next nine miles were more my style of terrain, a combination of single track, rocky terrain, loads of climbing and treacherous downhill stretches. These downhill stretches allowed me to showcase my weak ankles, which I have accepted as strength. I laughed to myself as I thought of training runs where others told me of the impossibility of watching my feet while I run, ankles constantly flapping side to side, hitting the dirt.

I bounced back and forth between groups at this stretch and rolled into mile 17 aid station unscathed and about 15 minutes ahead of pace. No falls, no drama. However, I did begin to notice that the 2,000 feet of climbing was taking a toll on my body. As expected, my wife Traci was at the Washington Park aid station to fill my pack, get me a sandwich, and push me back onto the trail. With tired legs but good spirits, I came to the first significant water crossing of the day. I spotted a nice log to cross on, but my weak legs landed in the hard-flowing water. Turning my first water crossing into a mild swim, I climbed out of the creek and headed up the hill.

Mile 17-33 consisted of a burn area, highlighted by no shade, thick sharp Manzanita bushes, a narrow trail, and 3,000 feet of climbing. With long grasses covering dead tree stumps and rocks littering the ground, I adjusted my mindset to maneuver carefully, yet swiftly. I told myself if I could make it through this stretch unscathed (both mentally and physically), I could take it down a notch at the next aid station.

I began to really feel my stride for the first time in the day when I arrived at the aptly named Hell's Gate. Hell's Gate is a very remote aid station that is only accessible by four-wheel-drive off-road vehicles so there was no option to receive aid from my crew. The unseasonably warm 80-degree temperature began to take its toll on me. I mentally prepared for the next eight or so miles in the open burn area, and longed for shade.

Cow bells rang from below as another runner and I rounded the corner. A volunteer yelled down to others that number 43 was coming down, get his drop bag ready. I looked over the side of the hill and recognized the aid station from a video of previous races. I began to yell a little and I was excited to know I had the first 33 miles down, 30 minutes ahead of pace! It was only 12:03 pm as I rolled into the aid station, and while I had taken some significant falls during the race, I felt really strong. I ate a few orange slices, had half of a turkey-and-cheese sandwich followed by some Tums (to keep the sandwich down). Then I was ready to head out for my next challenge. Traci was also there to quickly fill my bag with Gatorade and give me a water bottle to carry. We didn't need to discuss it; we both knew I had the longest, hardest stretch of the course coming up. With a quick kiss from her, I was on my way out of the Fish Hatchery aid station. I felt great and was in good spirits as families cheered for me when I left the aid station. The ultra-community shone as people I had never met offered words of encouragement and boosted my spirits, pushing me out of the aid station.

Arizona has a dry heat, but as I made the next climb I was soaked and baking in the sun. I struggled to keep my feet moving up the 1,800-foot, 11-mile slope. This never-ending hill had quickly become the bane of my existence. The temperature topped out at 89 degrees in Northern Arizona, and I had managed to suck every last drop of water there was out of the two bottles I carried. To my surprise, none of the other participants in the race had passed me, even though I had dropped from a 10- to a 21- minute per mile pace. They must have been suffering as well.

My mind was playing tricks on me, so when I saw a group of

people holding water towards the top of the hill, I hoped it wasn't a mirage. "Do you need water?" I heard one of the volunteers ask. Thank God they were real.

The crusty white layer of salt coating my face gave me a ghostly appearance. I was dehydrated, thirsty, bloated, and utterly exhausted from already traveling 39 miles on the Zane Grey 50 Mile ultra-marathon course. The volunteers offered to fill my empty bottles with water, but cautioned me that it was filtered water from the nearby creek. At that time, I couldn't have cared less that the water came from a creek. I'm certain that if the water had been brown with all kinds of floating creatures in it, I still would have guzzled it down. The few moments of company and the cold water gave me just the strength I needed to tackle the next stretch of the course. One of the volunteers explained that the next aid station would be about 4.6 miles down the trail and wished me good luck.

As I continued along the trail, my legs got heavy and turned to bricks. My breathing became so labored it reminded me of a dog panting in the summer heat. I decided to hike for a while in hopes that I could flush out my legs and regain a steady breathing pattern. Nothing was working. I would walk about 100 feet before buckling over, hands on knees, to prevent my body from hitting the ground. I decided to sit down for only a minute to get my breathing under control. Inching along at this pace was getting me nowhere, but maybe just a minute's rest would do me wonders. This turned out to be a horrible idea. As soon as I sat down, I became nauseous and got the spins. I felt like I was back in college, drunk after one of my brother's frat parties. I rummaged through my bag for a magic pill that would make my nausea and the pain in my body go away. What I found was a few Tums and a couple of salt tablets. I figured nothing could make me worse, so I threw them in my mouth. The Tums crumbled like chalk and stuck to the insides of my cheek. I unhooked my bag from my shoulders, removed my iPod earphones and sprawled out on the ground. I was right in the middle of the trail and still out in the direct sunlight. Minutes passed and I still had no relief from the pain. I realized I might not get up for a while so I pulled myself to the side of the trail to be out of the way of passing runners. I couldn't sit up because each time I would try, it would send shooting pain through my hips. Using a handful of leaves and a couple large rocks that were within reach, I built a makeshift bed and closed my eyes.

When I first set out to run an ultra-marathon (any race longer than the typical 26.2 marathon distance), a fellow ultra-runner provided me with this warning, "During an ultra you will experience the highest of highs, but you will also be challenged and have to overcome the lowest of lows. Be prepared." As I lay on the side of the historic Highline Trail, miles from the finish line of the Zane Grey 50 Mile race, I understood what he meant. This was definitely a very low point in the race for me. However, the excruciating pain I felt on the sidelines of the race that day paled in comparison to the pain I had endured 18 months earlier on the morning of September 23rd, 2008.

Chapter 2: The Phone Call That Changed My Life

The caller ID on my phone told me it was my brother Bryan calling at four o'clock in the morning. Why was he calling so early? I assumed he had misdialed or was traveling and had maybe lost track of time. Groggy with sleep, I considered not answering, but eventually I picked up the phone to hear what he had to say.

In times like these, the caller has no choice but to be frank. From the other line I heard, "Jay, Dad had a pulmonary embolism this morning, was taken to the hospital and they were not able to save him."

In utter disbelief, I sank to the floor and screamed, "No! No! No!"

Pain paralyzed my body and I dropped the phone. My dad, the man who had always believed in me, was gone at the age of 58. This cut so deep. It hurt like no pain I have ever felt before.

I began to shake. I continued screaming uncontrollably which woke Traci and our daughter, Petra.

Tears poured from my eyes. I could barely stop crying but had to because I knew in a few moments I would need to compose myself in order to talk to my mom. I briefly spoke to my sister Jill before she put my mom on the line. When I heard my mom's voice, my throat closed up and I couldn't say a thing. In a trembling tone, she told me she was sorry for my loss. For a moment we just sat silently and cried together. I was distraught for her and the rest of my family and I knew that no words would ease any of our pain. What was my mom going to do without my dad? How was she going to make it? They had been married for 36 years and had one of the strongest relationships I have ever seen.

This horrible news also came at a time when I was starting to really be happy and excited about life. Traci had given birth to our daughter Petra just nine months earlier and I was a dad myself for the first time. As I became a father I gained a better appreciation for everything my dad had done for me and it was in this moment that I wished so badly that I could tell him how much it all meant to me and that I loved him one more time.

***

We flew to Michigan that morning from Arizona. The funeral would be a few days later. I was numb to what had happened.

When the day came to lay my dad to rest, it was only the second time in my life I had stepped into a funeral home. I hated the feeling and the quiet awkwardness that filled the room when I walked through the doors. My family waited for the funeral director to call us in to see his body and have a moment with him before the extended family and friends would arrive. I tried to tell myself that this wasn't real but I knew that as soon as I walked through the doors to the viewing area, my mind and body were going to crumble.

The room was warm but I knew when I felt his hand it would be cold and lifeless. Not wanting to believe that it was him lying there, I took a quick look and walked out of the room. He looked peaceful but I wasn't in the right mind to stay and say my goodbyes. Not yet.

The room was filled with pictures of my dad. There were old childhood pictures, some from when we were growing up in Michigan, and most recent were those from our amazing trip to Hawaii just a few weeks earlier. The room where we were to have his service was a rather large room, but it was quickly filled from wall to wall with family and friends.

They shared wonderful stories about him. Even co-workers he hadn't been in contact with for 20 years came to pay their respects. He made such an impression on the lives of everyone he met. One by one they all came up to our family and raved about the man he was. I could feel their pain with each hug and tear shed. But with each compliment they shared about my dad, my sorrow slowly turned to joy. It was so comforting to know that one person could touch so many.

The funeral was very difficult for me as my brother and I carried the casket into the church in preparation for one last goodbye. As we made our way to the front of the church and I saw all the faces that had come to honor his life, tears streamed down my face. Some people fear public speaking but for me it comes naturally, especially when talking about something or someone I love. Giving a eulogy for one of my parents is by far the toughest thing I've ever had to do. Standing at the front of the viewing room, looking at the sad faces and trying to tell stories of the man he was without breaking down, was going to be difficult. I chose to follow my brother and sister so I could have a few minutes to gather myself together before talking. The night before I had outlined what I wanted to say but after Jill finished speaking, I decided I wanted to ad lib. Standing up in front of this large audience, I felt excited to tell stories of my dad, who I had endearingly called T since I was a young child.

When I was six years old my dad and I formed a special bond at the University of Michigan football games. As a child, I was always so excited when fall would come because that meant I got to tag along with my dad to the University of Michigan football games every Saturday. He always met friends and co-workers at tailgate parties before the game. It was at these get-togethers that I would hear my dad's co-workers and friends say to him, "Hey Touchdown", or "How are you, TD?" I didn't understand why they called him that. His name was Tom Danek. I asked my dad why they called him that and he just said that giving nicknames was a "cool" way of referring to friends instead of calling them by their first name. Since this was a cool thing to do, I wanted my own nickname for him. I woke one morning and started referring to my dad as T. I thought it would be great to have a special nickname between him and his kids, so I started calling him T. We could have called him TD like his co-workers, which was short for his full name, but I liked to keep things simple so I shortened his first name from Tom to T. At first I thought this would go over about as well as referring to your parents by their first names, but he was receptive. It didn't bother him and he wasn't one of those parents who was trying to be the cool parent. Instead he saw this as a special nickname from his kids. It didn't take long for family and friends to catch on to the name and start to call him T. He never uttered a word about us kids calling him T; in fact I know he loved it by the smile on his face every time we said his name.

I stood up and talked for about 10 minutes and while I wanted to cry the entire time, I fought back the tears and I told stories about him that made everyone laugh, cry, and remember the man who had been there for so many.

After the mass was dismissed, I walked over to my dad at the altar. I wanted to hold his hand just one last time and tell him how much I loved him. I shook as the feeling of emptiness took over my body. His hand was cold, but in that last moment with him I could feel his spirit telling me everything would be okay.

The flight home to Arizona was extremely difficult for me because I knew when I called home to say that our flight had landed, my dad would not answer. He would not be able to answer the phone like he usually did every afternoon when I would call to talk to him about Michigan football or to ask him crucial questions on how to be a good father.

Weeks went by and when I knew no one would be at home in Michigan, I would call my parents' house to hear his voice on the answering machine. I think his voice comforted my mom as well because she left it on the answering machine for more than a year after he passed.

But it wasn't the same. I knew I was never going to be able to talk to him again and it killed me inside and out. I wondered whether, if I hadn't pushed my dad to get on a plane to Hawaii, it would have made a difference. The doctors had told him to be careful when flying and walking a lot. He had a previous blood clot condition and these activities could make it flare up. Had we walked too much on the island?

I had no idea how to move on with my life without feeling angry, scared and guilty. I kept thinking about how just a few weeks before this awful day, I had been with my dad in Hawaii on a trip he had called "the best vacation your mom and I have ever been on."

***

My wife, Traci, and I have been fortunate enough to be able to vacation in Maui every year for the past few years. It is something we look forward to all year and 2008 brought even more excitement because this would be our first trip with our 8 ½-month-old daughter, Petra. Each year when we planned the trip, Traci and I would ask my parents to join us as well. Usually our invitation was declined—not because they didn't want to spend time with us, but because they felt the travel distance would completely wear them out. Living out west in Arizona makes it very convenient for Traci and me to fly to Maui, but since my parents live in Michigan, it would mean a full day of travel plus a six-hour time difference. It must have been the addition of their beautiful new granddaughter to the trip that changed their minds, because this year they finally decided to join us. I was so excited! I knew it would be an amazing trip.

My mom and dad handled the flight well and we all finally arrived at Kahului Airport in Maui. My dad, T, was normally a very calm, cool and collected individual, but as soon as he stepped off the plane and felt the trade winds blow, he came alive with excitement. I suggested that we pick up a few items at the store before heading to our condo. As my mom and Traci finished shopping, I watched T roam around the store, looking anxious to get out of there and see the sights. When I reflect on that moment, I think it was funny because it seemed like our roles in life were reversed for a little while. Growing up, I had always been the anxious child with no patience and T had always stayed calm. Now, he was bouncing off the walls with excitement, causing me to assume the cool, calm and collected role. As we left the store, I took a few moments to explain "Maui time" to my dad.

The first rule of "Maui time" is to turn your phone off and, whatever pace you would go on the mainland, cut it in half. There is nothing fast about being on the islands. From the stores to the service, everyone is on Maui time. The good thing about this is that no one gets angry with the slow pace and most people adapt to it. It is as if the beauty of the island is enough to temporarily stop time long enough to allow you to really enjoy it. Traci and I first learned about Maui time when we went to the big island of Hawaii two years earlier and sat through a horrible time-share presentation the hotel tricked us into.

We listened intently for an hour about the resort and its amenities but then at the very end of the presentation we were told something that I still think about every time we go. The presenter discussed the difference between the island tourist and those who live there. He said the only way to really see the islands is to slow down while driving and shut out the outside world. If someone comes up fast behind you on the road, simply roll down your window and wave them on. They are either locals in a hurry to get to work or they are tourists who can't slow their brain down and enjoy the islands. He said if you can't relax here, then you can't relax anywhere. I always had a problem relaxing before this trip but after hearing him talk, I was able to understand exactly what he meant.

I began to work on my patience, which to this day is still very low. I found that the islands bring something out in me which allows me to be a little more patient with each visit. I don't expect to move fast, I expect the days to be long and slow and I hope to take in all the sights. The speed limits on the roads from the store to the condo were no faster than 40 miles an hour. There was a constant stream of cars pulling over to the side of the road to take pictures of the amazing landscape, but this didn't bother me, because I knew not to be in a hurry. The colors reign supreme on this island and are invigorating to the spirit. I tried to take them all in. There were deep purple flowers, and gorgeous green landscapes. Women wore bright pink hues of the hibiscus flowers in their hair and the beautiful blue ocean stretched out as far as the eye could see.

After arriving at the condo, we walked into our oasis on the ocean. Just as they were on our drive, the sights near our condo were incredible. But the day had been long, and soon my dad realized he needed to rest. He walked out onto the lanai and put his leg up on a chair, leaning back to enjoy the Maui trade winds. The travel time alone would be tiring to anyone, but my dad also had a medical issue which caused him to need to rest his leg. He had been bitten by a brown recluse spider about 15 years earlier which resulted in a blood clot in his left leg. For years, he was prescribed Coumadin to help with circulation, but since no issues had occurred since his long hospital stay years earlier, the doctors had taken him off the medicine, directing him to wear a compression sock on his leg instead. This was especially important whenever he knew he would be flying or if he intended to walk for long periods of time. He would experience occasional flare-ups in his leg, but nothing that simple elevation wouldn't quickly correct. Seeing him elevate his leg now, I knew he must have been feeling a flare-up. T was always a good sport and laughed any time his family, including myself, referred to his bad leg as his "trunk." I found it hard to watch him have to wear the compression sock in the hot humidity of Maui, but he took his circumstances in stride, never complaining. This is something I always envied about him and have since tried to emulate.

After a brief rest by the ocean, it didn't take my parents long to adjust to Maui time. They were in paradise, enjoying every moment they were spending with Petra. Petra was enamored with her grandparents from the moment she saw them. All kids should get the opportunity to grow up with their grandparents and, since we lived 2,000 miles apart, this was only the third time they had ever met. Some babies tend to cling to their parents but she lit up every time my mom or dad would hold her. Traci and I had been wondering for a couple months now when she would start crawling and damn if it wasn't 30 seconds after we arrived at the condo in Maui that she decided to try. We were all sitting down relaxing and Petra was darting back and forth across the floor, bringing huge smiles to all our faces. I was happy we could share this milestone with my parents.

We went into this trip with complete relaxation in mind and every day was scheduled to include nothing but watching the waves and taking in the sun. One of the keys to Maui is to not plan a ton of activities every day, but instead just relax and take in the amazing scenery. Where the roads or ocean took us each day is where we would go, never keeping to a specific plan.

That being said, my dad did have a couple of things he wanted to do during his time there so we made sure to look into those activities. One of his goals was to drive the road to Hana. This was something Traci and I had heard about on previous trips but had never done. So when T brought it up, we were on board with the idea.

We soon found out that the Hana highway is one of the most beautiful, while also nerve-wracking, 44 miles of road one might ever travel. You must exercise an extreme amount of caution on the more than 200 hairpin turns of mostly single-lane roads with two-way traffic. With tourists everywhere snapping photos of the rain forests and high waterfall alerts, a compact car would make for a safe ride along this road. Unfortunately, our rented Cadillac Escalade wasn't exactly compact.

From the back seat I was constantly letting T know that this was the car ride from hell. Petra was crying and the locals were yelling at us to let them by on the road, so the peaceful trip to Hana was turning out to be anything but peaceful. Even so, T never seemed to be concerned with anyone around us. He didn't let the other impatient drivers get to him and slowly, over the length of that car ride, I began to relax because he was relaxed. I eventually followed his lead, accepting things I could not change: taking them in stride. We were given a large car and it took up most of the road and there wasn't much we could do about it except turn around and go home but nobody wanted to do that, so, we inched along, pulling over several dozen times to check out the scenery and take a picture or two. After several of these breaks, I started to let go of the feelings of anxiety that were trying to wreck my day. I was finally able to take in the sights and sounds of the Hana highway and it was thanks to T's calm composure.

My parents had the relaxing vacation they had always dreamed of, got to spend time with us, and became more acquainted with their new granddaughter. Days after returning, T called to recap the previous week. He said he had loved it and that we should all plan on going back the next year. I couldn't have agreed with him more. Traci and I had been to Hawaii several times but this was by far the best trip we had ever had there and I was already looking forward to reserving the condo again for the next year.

Chapter 3: Finding Strength

I lay vulnerable on the side of the Highline trail at the Zane Grey 50 for what seemed like hours. Happy memories of T seemed to be the only thing that was keeping me going. When 10 minutes had passed, a runner and his pacer caught up to me. Seeing my pale, seemingly lifeless body sprawled out on the side of the trail, the two asked whether I needed any help. Not wanting to get pulled from the race, I mumbled that I was okay. "Just enjoying a break," I said. Twenty minutes and 12 more runners later, I began to worry I might have to make the decision to call for help. The problem was that I was still 3.5 miles from the aid station. I had no water, and Gatorade tasted horrible. Even if my mind could convince my body to quit, I would have to either walk to the aid station or be hauled out by helicopter.

The final runner I encountered while sulking in equal parts pity and dehydration happened to have a doctor as a pacer. I felt like I had altitude sickness. I was dizzy, and felt extreme pain through my legs and hips. The pacer asked if he could take my pulse and check me out quickly to see if he should send help. Apparently I passed all the tests, so he told me I could continue when I was ready and offered me a drink called "Recovery." Sipping on the recovery drink for a minute gave me the boost I needed to head back out on the trail. I tried to shift my thoughts to a happier place so I wouldn't keep focusing on the pain in my legs.

I remembered Hawaii and the permanent smile on T's face as he soaked in the beauty the island had to offer. I thought of my wife Traci and beautiful daughter Petra playing at the beach. Those happy thoughts were enough to alter my mood and somehow they seemed to lessen the anguish I was feeling as I carried on down the trail to the next aid stations.

I pulled my Garmin out of my pocket for a distance reading and realized that my 30-minute nap had dropped the pace of my last mile to a 49-minute pace! I knew I had to make up time. I quickly made some mental calculations and reassured myself that with 10 miles left, I could easily finish in less than 13 hours if I just pushed it a little.

About a quarter of a mile from the next aid station, I saw Traci running down the hill toward me. She had been tipped off by a few runners who had passed me lying in the ditch. They told her I was not doing well and needed fluids. Traci was so happy to see me standing upright and I was overjoyed to see a familiar face. I knew now that I would be able to finish the race. She had a bottle for me, but funny enough, I couldn't take a drink from her without being disqualified until I reached the aid station. Since it was only a quarter-mile away, I carried on and finally got relief at the mile 44 aid station.

I had spent 10 hours alone with my thoughts, but now I was allowed a pacer. Tere joined me from mile 44 on with a job to motivate me to finish no matter what. She helped push me to attack the downhill portions, told me to keep moving when we approached an uphill section, and filled the now vacant space between my ears with encouraging thoughts. I focused on just moving each foot forward and listened to Tere for the next six miles. Blinded by excruciating pain from the blisters on my toes and perhaps also the salty sweat that had accumulated in my eyes, I barely noticed as my watch beeped at the 50-mile mark. But I suddenly heard voices yelling, "Runner!"

A runner I certainly was, and I was also seconds away from crossing the finish line!

It brought me back to reality. I had just completed one of the hardest 50-mile races in the country, if not the hardest. But it was much more challenging than my first and I had overcome some very low moments along the way.

That day, I left the vision of a man I once was out on the side of that trail. There had been times in my life when I would have easily given up and not continued on. But things were different now. I had the thoughts of my dad motivating me. Somewhere on that course I grew into a stronger, more grateful person for the opportunity to be alive. Each struggle became a challenge I wanted to complete. This was a huge stepping stone for me in my healing. It built up my confidence and made me appreciate all that I have.

It had taken a tragedy in my life to bring me to this point. I had reached my ultimate low only to be topped by the ultimate high I felt as I saw the loves of my life, Traci and Petra, standing at the finish line cheering me on. I began to see myself as the husband and father T would have been proud of. My new passion for ultra-running could not be tamed. I immediately started to explore what training looked like and what dates were available for my first 100-mile race!

Chapter 4: Why Ultras?

In order to fully explain my transformation from the impatient man I once was to the calmer and appreciative man I am today, it is best for me to describe the amount of patience and tenacity it takes to complete what has now become one of my life passions—the ultra-marathon.

The ultra-marathon race is unlike anything else in this world. In a 5K or 10K race, many thoughts play through a runner's mind at the start: Will I hit my splits? Will I be able to stay on pace? Who is my competition? Such runners are always wondering what to expect. It is very rare, though, that they start the race not knowing whether they will finish it. This is different than an ultra. When you toe the line of a hundred-mile race, it is much harder to have any expectations at all. No one can ever quite predict your outcome and 50 percent of racers never even reach the finish line. When you sign up for an ultra, it is not a race against time; it is a race against your mind.

To put it into perspective, you would likely cringe if you drove past a road sign that read 95 miles to your next destination. But what if you saw a similar sign letting you know you still had 95 miles to *run*? Where would you shift your thoughts to keep your mind off those remaining miles you must fight through? During the long journey, you might face a number of different elements. You might run up and over snow-covered mountains, travel down a trail leading into a dark forest of pine trees and eventually climb up a road in the hot California desert. How long can you stay positive, what will make you crack and how will you conquer each challenge? Which eye-opening experience will mold you into a stronger, more grateful person? And how many new things will you learn about yourself along the way?

So what exactly is an ultra-marathon? An ultra-marathon is considered to be any distance run that is farther than a marathon. Distances start at 50K or 31 miles. The thought that comes to most people's minds when they hear that races of these distances exist is, "Why would anyone ever want to run 31 miles or longer? I don't even like to drive 31 miles!" It is even harder for most to understand the hundred-mile race.

The start of a hundred-mile race gives runners the feeling of being born again. The shining beams of light seem unfamiliar while you are standing in the dark, looking over the horizon. As you peer out into the distance, you might make out a mountain you will scale later that day or you might see what looks like a trail that will need to be carefully navigated. As you wait for race instructions, you know quite well that you are about to embark on a journey of the mind and an inevitable fight with your own body.

Some call ultra-marathons life-changing, I also see them as eye-opening. A phrase that I saw during a race in Texas plays through my mind every time I line up for one of these races: "No matter how good or bad you feel right now, it will change in a minute." From experience, I know nothing could be closer to the truth. It is not uncommon during one of these races to be running along with a joyful spirit, singing to the lyrics of your favorite song, and then unexpectedly to be overcome with a painful stomach cramp. Or your legs might suddenly give way on you, feeling heavy as though you've been running on them for months straight. A small blister between your toes or rolling your ankle at mile 70 might be the difference between the glory of being handed a hundred-mile buckle at the finish line and having to walk off the course early with an injury. There is no prize for running 70 miles out of 100; in fact, you can run 99 miles, but if you don't cross the finish line you will receive a "Did Not Finish" printed next to your name, no different from a participant who drops out at mile one.

If the notion of pain and suffering along the way and the thought of not finishing one of these races do not stop you, you might begin training hard to prepare. Once you eventually sign up and your family and friends find out you did this willingly, they will probably ask you why you are doing this. I've spoken to many runners who say they do it for the high and the endorphins that come along with running. While the "runner's high" can be addicting, this is not what attracted me to the sport. For me, running is healing.

Chapter 5: Seeking Refuge From My Mind

Months went by after T died, and I was at a complete loss. I wasn't sure how to move forward. I had gone to therapy and sought advice from family and friends but nothing in life, not even Petra or Traci, seemed to make me smile for more than a few minutes at a time. I came to the conclusion that though therapy was helping, it was not the complete answer. I fell back into some old patterns. The knowledge that drinking would not relieve my pain seemed to have escaped me and I drank beer to numb my pain. My depression grew by the day.

I would wake each morning as if I was back in the nightmare of the day I received that call. When I wasn't awake, I would dream about it. I tried to escape the dream by taking prescription pills but found myself losing interest in everything around me. When one pill wouldn't work I would take two and hope for relief, but found none.

Life seemed to be a tremendous battle and when I wasn't tackling my own demons, I was seeking out arguments with my wife Traci. She was the one person who was doing everything to help me, and I knew it but I couldn't appreciate it because I was clouded with despair. Despite her fear for me on the inside, she remained calm and looked for ways to change my negative behaviors. Seeking help of family and friends, she tried to reach out to me and make me realize I was going to need to take things slowly. She knew we would get through this mess but I didn't want to hear it. I managed to find anger in situations where there was none. Traci never faltered. She continued to help me work through my grief and find positive ways to manage my pain, but my impatient nature didn't have the time. I wanted the situation to be resolved as fast as it had occurred but there clearly was no easy answer.

All the while, wrapped in my own sorrow, I never realized the pain Traci felt for losing her father-in-law. She would try and tell me just how hard the loss of my dad was for her but I was too selfish to see that it affected anyone but me.

Traci had had a special bond with my dad that started the day she walked through my front door asking to borrow a graphing calculator. If it wasn't for my dad, the two of us never would have gotten together. I would have continued to blow her off each time she called. It was actually T, the man with patience, who saw how incredible Traci was right away. He knew that if I didn't wake up and pursue her she would be swept away by someone else and I would miss my chance. I'm so grateful that when he provided this bit of advice I decided to listen. I often hear people say men look to marry someone who resembles their mom. I think in this case, I actually married someone whose character resembles my dad's.

Traci's character mirrors my dad's in so many ways. She has the same level of patience, she is highly intelligent and like my dad, the little things in life never irritate her like they do me. It is my mom and I who are always anxiety-driven and impatient.

My friends would tell me they were worried about me; Traci would suggest I join a sports team or find an activity that would ease my mind. I just had no idea what I was going to find that would get me out of my funk. I really didn't believe that anything would work and part of me didn't even want to try. I now weighed 275 pounds, had put on 45 pounds since my dad passed away, had no passion for anything, and was angry. I wasn't angry with anyone in particular; I was angry with myself.

I needed a change and Traci was determined to help me get through this situation. Again, she was my rock. I picked fights with those I loved, over nothing, never leaving me with a sense of relief. It merely brought on more resentment and anger. It is tough to explain how anger sets in when you lose someone so close, but I found it to be one of the hardest steps in the grieving process.

I would go home and drink eight to 10 beers just to take the pain away so I could go to sleep, hoping the next day would be better. It never was. My depression grew deeper, leaving me to wonder how I would continue on. While I didn't have any drastic thoughts about doing harm to myself, I wondered how I would carry on and be as good a father to my daughter that my dad was to me.

After seven months in this depressed state, my birthday rolled around. Needless to say, I had zero excitement for the day to arrive. This was especially true considering T's birthday was the day before mine—something we always shared.

When I woke up that morning, Traci handed me an envelope which contained my birthday present. It was a gift certificate to an exercise boot camp that would start the next week. I would rank this gift right up there with buying your wife an ironing board or vacuum for her birthday. I was angry about it, not because she thought I was overweight—I knew I was—but because there was slim hope that it was going to be something fun and exciting that could help get me out of my current state of depression. I couldn't believe that this was what she had bought me for my birthday. She had been repeatedly telling me that I needed to do something with myself and this was her answer? At the time, I couldn't think of anything worse that she could have given me.

Looking back, what I thought was a lousy birthday gift was actually one of the best gifts I had ever received because it jump-started the next phase of my life.

After a week of going back and forth about just giving the program a try and seeing what would happen, I finally decided I would show up and complete the full session, whether I enjoyed it or not.

The first day of class was interesting. I showed up for my first class to find a group of fit ladies with their yoga mats, pretty water bottles, and weights lined up waiting for the instructor. I felt like they were all looking at the large man with no neck who was so overweight and unfit he would probably collapse in the middle of the class.

The class started with some simple stretching, but when you are so large that you can barely touch your knees, let alone your toes, there is no such thing as "simple stretching." At this point, even stretching was frustrating and humiliating. My head immediately sank as those around me took on their crazy yoga poses. For once, I was not the standout athlete in the bunch. If this were a game where the captains picked the team members, there would be no doubt I would have been chosen last and even this would have been out of pity.

Back in high school and college, even when I had put on a little bit of weight, I had still been still athletic enough to compete on a high level on the basketball court and on the baseball field. Yet the gym and running were completely different. These aspects of fitness did not interest me. Nor did I care if I could run a mile or bench press half my weight. I always found it to be ridiculous that people would waste time on a sport such as running that would ultimately be the demise of their knees. Similarly, I looked at weightlifters as people who spent time lifting so they could squeeze into a shirt two sizes too small to play the part of club bouncer look-alike. I thought, seriously, don't your arms get tired from holding them out to the side like that all the time; wouldn't it be easier and more comfortable if they lay normally against your sides? I guess these were things that eased my mind about being overweight. Fit people were out of my league. In reality, it was much easier to make fun of someone than to actually get out there and try it myself.

After some initial stretches, we were told to run across the soccer field and back. The object was not to run fast but to be able to make it there and back without keeling over and dying. Let's be realistic: a soccer field is only 60 yards across, so I needed to run 120 yards. At first glance it seemed like an impossible feat. I had absolutely no chance of making it halfway across the field one time, let alone running there and back. While I had never been a runner at any point in my life and this seemed to be impossible, I found it funny how many of the ladies were complaining about the distance we were going to have to run. This actually gave me some motivation to get out there and prove to myself that I was not as big of a slug as I thought.

Lugging around an extra 100 pounds really begins to take a toll on the body and mind when you are trying to do something semi-athletic. Running a measly 120 yards was no different, no matter how slow I was going. When I took my first few steps, I could barely picture myself making it to midfield. As I started to run and follow the group, I began to feel ashamed of the way I looked and had acted for the past seven months. It was as though hitting the wall while running a short distance opened my eyes and I started to see the light at the end of the tunnel. I wasn't quite sure just how far away the light was, but there was finally a light after all.

It was right then I decided to give life a chance and stop saying, "I can't." I changed that broken record playing in my mind to "I can." It had been so easy to sit there and say that I couldn't do something. I knew it would take real determination to decide to go after something and set a goal, but I was now finally ready for the challenge. Even though many people had tried, it was no one else's responsibility to help me make a change; it was something I had to conjure up from deep inside. I needed to make a change in my life and I knew it needed to happen sooner rather than later.

The fit yoga ladies with incredible bodies at boot camp were able to do all the exercises and I was so out of shape that lifting a 10-pound weight over my head left me winded and tired after a couple repetitions. I wasn't going to let it stop me even though it hurt because I knew deep down that what I was going through was temporary and I could change if I committed to it. To add further embarrassment, the instructor told me I should bring five-pound weights to class for the next session and then work my way up to 10 pounds. Seriously? These girls were 110 pounds, using 10-pound weights for drills. I was 275 pounds, using 5-pound weights? There was absolutely no way I was going to give in and show up with 5-pound weights for the next class. I remained stubborn but determined to get into shape.

Sometimes it is the little things like not being able to lift a weight that can help us make a change in life. While other times it takes a greater force, this sure was a pretty good place for me to start. I mean, what was next? Was I going to have to go back to using a little league bat for baseball?

Boot camp became a real test for me every Tuesday and Thursday. For the first month I didn't see much improvement in the way of weight loss, but was starting to feel a little fit. I was now able to run across the soccer field without taking a break. My next goal: running there and back without feeling like I would need oxygen. I started to notice an increase in my strength and my running form began to improve after a few more sessions.

Just being able to do the simplest exercises started to make going to the classes fun. The exercises seemed to be much easier once I grasped the concept of how to do them and why we were doing them. The girls were there to improve their nearly perfect bodies and I was there to figure out if this was a good start to healing my broken mental state.

Three weeks into boot camp, something happened that really could have derailed my progress. I noticed some contractors surveying the soccer field. Since I work in the grass (sod) business, I figured there was a good chance I would know the guys who were checking out the field. At closer look, I not only knew them, but one was a friend of mine who did a triple take as he saw me chug 20 yards behind the other boot camp participants. At first, he looked at me with the plain expression of "What is that guy doing?" and then a clearer, "Is that Jay out there?"

It was a humbling moment, leading me to one of two directions. I could either thrive, living in the moment and go explain to the men how participating in this class was my attempt to get back to reality, or I could curl up in embarrassment and hide behind the skinny ladies, hoping that they didn't see me and then lie about it later when they asked.

I was tired of not living, though, so I went with the first option and walked straight up to my colleagues. I wanted to show them the new and improved me. I wanted them to see how far I had come and how I was starting to be a more positive person. I was actually proud of what I was doing and while I was the slow, overweight guy running 20 yards behind the group, I was out there giving it my all and I took pride in my progress. I knew I was going to be razzed and it would be a joke every time I saw them in the future, but I knew the light was out there, which mattered more to me than a little joking among friends.

More importantly, Traci was starting to see a change in me mentally. She told me I seemed happier and I felt happier. So I began to embrace the power of change.

I finished the first session of boot camp and decided to sign up on my own for the next. There was no prodding or someone giving me a gift certificate to make myself thinner. I was committed to making myself happier. I didn't want to be the anchor my wife was dragging around. Worse yet, I didn't want Petra to grow up regretting the time she spent with me. Petra was just a year old now, but she really seemed to be a daddy's girl and always wanted to be by my side. There was no way that I was going to let this sweet little girl see me fail at anything, even if it was just boot camp.

The second session seemed quite different. In addition to the fit ladies, a group of equally fit men also flaunted their weights and flexibility. They all seemed to know each other, leaving me feeling like an outsider, even though I am a very outgoing person. I told myself it made no difference; I wasn't there to talk or make friends; I was there to lose weight.

The instructor asked what my goal was for this camp and I said I wanted to be down 40 pounds by the end of the session. While this was an extremely big goal for such a short amount of time, I truly thought I had it in me to lose the weight if I could just get a jump start. Besides the Atkins Diet, I was not well versed in the fad diets of the day. I loved to eat bread and other carbs, so basically starving my body of foods it loved wasn't going to work for me. I needed a plan and a diet but nothing out there seemed to be just right for me.

I came home one day and told Traci about an idea I had to cut back calories. This idea was really out there and no dietician in his or her right mind would ever tell someone to try what I did, but I wanted to give it a try. I had decided to design a plan that would not only limit my calorie intake but would speed up the weight loss. That evening I laid out my plan to Traci and she looked dumbfounded that anyone could possibly think this would work. She was working out with a nutritionist who gave other tips and told me what to cut out but I had a vision and this was my plan. Traci knew just how headstrong I was, and nothing she said was going to change my mind, so she let me have at it.

The diet began with the concept that I was never really big on eating breakfast and to me it was nothing more than wasted calories. While I enjoy the foods it offers, I never understood the calorie consumption that accompanied the meal. Even though most dieticians will tell you breakfast is the most important meal of the day, I planned to take my body to the limit and cut out all calories before 11 am. I would only eat lunch and dinner, and a small snack (if absolutely necessary). If I needed extra calories, they would come in the form of recovery drinks that would keep me full so I didn't feel the need to eat. The average male eats around 2,200 calories a day and I wanted to cut my intake to 1,500. On top of this, I planned to work out an hour a day, burning 500 calories, in an attempt to speed up my weight loss. (Have I mentioned my lack of patience yet?)

Most people wake up hungry and are looking for something right away but I have always been different. I found that as soon as I ate, I would eat the rest of the day. With this in mind, convincing myself to fast until 11 am versus 6 am, I would potentially cut out 1,000-plus calories a day.

Researching my theory further, I found many overweight or obese people starve themselves all day and then binge eat when they get home. Not wanting to starve my body for the day, I knew I needed to be very careful if I was going to execute this plan.

The second part of my diet had to do with the amount of red meat I was consuming on a daily basis. I was basically a carnivore and had seen no need for any plants in my diet. My aim was to flip flop this and only allow fruits and vegetables for lunch, and a sensible dinner. What constituted a sensible dinner? This could be chicken, turkey, pork, salad, vegetables, or fruit but it could not contain red meat. Frankly, I was starting to become grossed out by the bloody undercooked steaks I was regularly consuming, so I thought this would be the perfect way to incorporate lean meats into the diet. Most studies would probably tell you that white meats are only a little healthier than red, but this was my diet and it really had no rhyme or reason; it was all based on calorie consumption. Telling me a turkey burger contained 500 fewer calories than a bacon cheeseburger seemed to offer enough motivation to make sensible choices.

The final phase of the diet was to find a food I knew I couldn't live without. When posed this question, most people might say pizza, spaghetti, or chocolate, but to me it was (and always will be) pretzels. I have always liked a certain amount of salt in my diet and these were the healthiest option among junk foods. Eating a bag of potato chips was going to be far more disastrous to my waistline than eating a bag of pretzel goldfish. Besides, pretzels always seemed to fill me up faster than chips, so my three-part diet was complete. In order to make an item like pretzels semi-acceptable, I had to cut out all other junk food, strictly stick to fruits and vegetables, and I absolutely could not partake of any dessert. By no means was this going to be easy, but I was confident this was going to be the magic bullet and no one could tell me differently.

Now the big question became: what if I was wrong and this completely backfired in the other direction? What if I ended up gaining weight instead of losing weight? In addition to my self-prescribed diet, I amped up my boot camp. Instead of attending two days a week, I increased it to three days, remembering as many exercises as I could to complete on my own on my off days. On Thursdays we would do cardio workouts, which now seemed to resemble a cross-fit workout.

Slowly and surely my strength and coordination began to improve. I was starting to see my body change, but the scale was not indicating the fact that I was losing weight. I could see and feel it in my clothes, but what was wrong with that scale? It was that day after weighing myself four or five times in the matter of hours that Traci pulled the scale from the house and banned me from ever setting foot on it again. It seemed as though I had found a new addiction: weight loss. It was as if I quickly traded in all my antidepressants for a new stumbling block, getting in the way of living life. Why wasn't I losing weight? My body seemed toned and I could now run back and forth across the soccer field, but I didn't feel any skinnier.

As we approached the end of the second session, I went for my weigh-in with the instructor and I found myself down close to 25 pounds from when we started the original boot camp two months prior. Blown away by my results, I began to preach my diet to others, only to be met by strange looks.

I wasn't becoming arrogant, but I was becoming someone who completely believed in the system of boot camp combined with a crazy diet equaling weight loss. My ultimate goal was to get to around 220 pounds because I thought that was my optimal weight, even though the doctor's office charts insisted I should be around 200 pounds. What six-foot-four-inch male weighs 200 pounds? I thought I would look like a skeleton if I dropped below 220, but 220 came and went just a month later and now it was decision time. Was I going to try to keep up with the boot camp schedule by going two nights a week and working out at home or was I going to start to do something else?

Frankly, I was pretty tired of the same routine where I basically had all the exercises memorized. I felt I was essentially wasting my time and money by attending a class for something I could do at home. I was bored and starting to lose interest, so I went to Traci for other ideas. She rattled off hundreds of things I could do but none caught my attention.

Then Traci asked me to come outside to take a look at what was in our front yard. I followed her out front and really had no idea what she wanted me to look at. She pointed to the mountains and said that I should start hiking. It sounded pretty fun but I really had no experience with hiking nor did I have any gear. She told me how her group at boot camp hiked it once a month and it was really fun and relaxing. I was definitely willing to give it a try, especially since it was a cheap alternative to boot camp. The thought of being out in the mountains really intrigued me since it was a way to be away from most people, out of the way of the city, and because of the difficulty of the terrain, I wouldn't have to worry about running.

Chapter 6: McDowell Mountain Man

Every morning for the next month, I would head to the McDowell Mountains and hike/crawl the 4.3-mile Gateway Loop. The first week was tough and I struggled to maintain a normal breathing pattern on the climbs. At least each climb was short and went by quickly. The views upon reaching the top were fantastic and even though I was tired from my slow pace going up the side of the mountain, I felt accomplished for reaching the top. I sat on top of the same rock each and every morning and when I would get up I would smile, knowing that I was accomplishing something I had never even thought of doing in the past.

Because I needed to be done with my hike before work, it was often dark when I would reach the top. Perhaps it was the darkness coupled with the fact that I was completely alone on this great mountain that provided me a certain sense of safety with my feelings. It was here that I felt completely vulnerable and was able to start talking to T out loud as if he was by my side.

I would look out to the horizon and watch as the sun rose. The beautiful red and orange sunrise here in Arizona seemed to blanket the sky and also blanket me with peace. I would tell T about something special I had learned the day before or share a funny story about Petra. I knew that no matter what I said he wouldn't be able to respond, but somehow I knew he was always listening and that was enough for me.

With no fancy GPS watch to tell me when I was close to the top of the mountain, I started using landmarks such as a cactus or a large rock to help me identify how far I had gone on the trail. I knew it was 2.3 miles to the halfway point, so I would estimate that a certain cactus was one mile, a big rock two, etc. Soon, those landmarks also served as additional places on the mountain where I would take a moment to reflect on a special memory about T.

For two weeks, I would only hike the trail, pointing to my dad in heaven as I reached the top of the summit. But, then one morning, I noticed a few people on the trail who were running down the slopes. They looked fit, which was something I was striving for. So I figured,

"Why not give running down the mountain a try?"

That morning after spending 30 seconds talking to T at the top, I decided it was time to try running down. I hoped gravity would help me out and push me down with ease. The sign at the summit read 1.8 miles to the Gateway trailhead and my first goal was to make it all the way. I was only going to stop if absolutely necessary. Now, the funny thing was, I still had never run a single mile on a flat surface without stopping, so who was I to think that I was going to magically pull off a 1.8-mile run down rocky terrain without stopping?

I was impatient and liked to do things my way so I took off like a bat out of hell. I pumped my arms and lifted my knees and tried to imagine myself with perfect running form.... that is, until I reached a tenth of a mile into the run, where I began wheezing, felt completely out of breath, and like I was having an asthma attack.

I felt the disappointment of the first boot camp cycle all over again. Why couldn't I do it? What was worse was that this time my feelings of inadequacy were compounded by the fact that I had lost weight and my diet had improved, so this should have been easier for me to complete than the 120-yard jog across the soccer field. I couldn't understand why my physical fitness wasn't getting any better.

Completely flustered, I walked the rest of the way down, shame weighing my head down low.

I came home that morning and, as she always did, Traci asked how my hike had been. I gave a real short answer that she didn't want to hear. I was angry I wasn't able to run like I had hoped and I told her walking up and down the mountain was useless. "No one loses weight from hiking," I said. I always enjoyed the times talking to my dad on each hike, but I also had a goal in mind to lose more weight and hiking was not delivering results. I needed to figure out how to run if I was ever going to lose any more pounds.

Naturally, she handled this just like my dad and told me to take it easy. Seeing that my interest had now turned to running, she explained to me some different running techniques she had read about. She told me she was also interested in running. She went on to tell me that one of the things on her bucket list of activities to do before she dies was to run a full marathon. A full marathon! I just wanted to run 1.8 miles so I could tell myself I could do it.

The next morning I was determined to conquer that downhill stretch. With all my might I started to run and I made it no farther than a tenth of a mile again before I had to stop and take a drink. Was it the temperature or was it that my body just wasn't conditioned to running? I really had no idea, but this time I didn't view stopping as failure. I looked at it as a step in the right direction.

I developed a plan to run another tenth of a mile and then another. I would just keep going until I needed to take a break and hopefully at some point it would get easier. By the end of that loop I had run five different sections of trail. Each section was about a tenth of a mile long. This was progress and I was happy to realize that I had just run half a mile during the 4.3-mile hike. I had never run a half mile before in my life!

Each morning I would go out with the goal of increasing the interval distance just a little bit, until finally running that entire downhill stretch seemed to come as easy to me as hiking it had been. I wasn't flying down the mountain by any means, but I was clicking off nine- to 10-minute miles going downhill, which was much better than the 17 minutes a mile it took me to go uphill.

For the better part of a month I tried to improve my performance from the day before. Eventually my nine- to 10-minute miles downhill became eight-minute miles. I was cutting my hiking time by a third, which allowed me to sleep in a little bit longer in the morning.

I wanted to learn to run the uphill portions too, so I started researching uphill running online. It talked about breathing through your nose and taking short fast steps. I read that having quick feet while going uphill would use less energy and keep my breathing intact because I would not be pushing myself beyond my limits. Before I could run uphill, I knew I needed to figure out the best way to stride in the flat areas and how I was going to improve on the rocks. My ankles were flopping side to side in my running shoes, so I decided it was time to invest in a good trail shoe.

I really didn't know what I was looking for in a shoe except that I wanted a little more stability for my wobbly ankles. I went into the local running shop and they put me on a treadmill to watch me run for a few minutes. Within moments of starting they were pointing to the monitor and talking about how badly I pronate.

When you over-pronate, you basically are running on the insides of your feet and losing all sense of balance. This seemed to be a problem for most people around me in the store, but they said mine was extremely bad and I needed to get the Brooks Cascadia trail shoe.

This bright yellow-and-black shoe was the ugliest thing I had ever seen and it seemed to weigh twice as much as the running shoes I was wearing, yet it was incredibly comfortable. The pillow-like feeling of this new shoe left me feeling propped up higher than my previous shoe.

I couldn't have been more excited to get out to the trails the next morning and try out the latest and greatest shoe on the market. I don't really know if I expected the shoe to carry me up the hill or I was going to feel something magical, but the moment I hit the trails, I felt like I had better control of my feet. For the first time since I had started hiking, I wasn't feeling every sharp, pointy rock stabbing me mid-foot as I struck it. My stride almost immediately began to change and I felt myself running toward the rocks instead of running away from them.

This loop started with 2.5 miles of uphill which I would have to hike and then I could run the 1.8-mile downhill stretch. I kept working on it, all the while talking to T every time I reached the saddle of Gateway. I would point to him in the sky, and run down the hill. After a few weeks of this routine, I decided it was time to try to run some of the hills. I figured it was only about 1,000 feet of vertical gain over the loop, so it shouldn't be that tough, but man it was. I would run, walk, run, walk.

Yet I was soon running the whole loop, only to stop at the top for a brief second to talk to T. I would count the days in a row I did it, how many miles I was running per week, and how much weight I was losing, but what I wasn't counting was how good it made me feel. I was back to being the person I knew I could be: a good dad, husband, and friend. My attitude was changing before my eyes and it had nothing to do with weight loss; it was all mental. I had an escape every day, a place I could talk to T, my best friend, and it was a way to honor him.

Every day I would tell myself, "He is so proud of you." My mom still says this to me. He would always let me know when he was proud of me, and I loved accomplishing things that would make him proud. I believe he is still looking down and smiling at my accomplishments today.

I think we all need an escape from the hectic moments in life. Whether your escape is yoga, running, sports, or even just reading a good book, it is nice to know that you can flee life's daily routines for just a little while and enjoy something you are really passionate about. This is what running became for me. It wasn't that I wanted to be alone every day; I just liked a few moments atop the mountain with my dad. Weeks became months of running in the McDowell's.

An issue arose as we approached a planned trip to Italy. I was excited to go on the trip and the last thing I wanted to do was compromise the vacation by worrying about running every day. So I made the conscious decision that I would not run the entire time we were there. This was harder than it seems. Since running had become my sanctuary, I had the itch to get out there and run through the streets of Rome. My mind toyed with the idea of waking up early and running each day while on vacation. At the same time I also felt like I had become a stronger runner before I left, so not running for 10 days wasn't going to make or break me. I'd pick it back up when I got home.

But the last few days of the trip, I could feel myself starting to worry again. I would lie in the hotel and worry about the future without my dad in my life. I didn't want to fall back into the mental anguish I had felt before. I also had a fear that I would gain all my weight back quickly and become a drain again on Traci. It's funny how the mind works.

Traci could tell something was on my mind, so we talked about it. Running can take hours depending on how far you might choose to go. I explained to my wife that I was concerned that in order to stay happy and keep running it might mean that it would take up more family time than she or Petra was used to and I certainly didn't want her to feel alienated by my newfound hobby. I know many couples who struggle when one person finds something they love to do and it takes up a large amount of their free time. I was so relieved when Traci told me she understood me and encouraged me to keep running. She said it was good for me and that for the first time since my father's passing, I was happy and fun to be around. She would rather have less time with happy Jay than more time with the previous depressed version of me. She was not going to ask me to stop and would support me in whatever I wanted to do.

Chapter 7: Honoring T with 923 Days of Running

Traci, Petra and I returned home from our trip to Italy in March 2010. I had been running every day prior to our trip, but during the trip I had not run at all and I was itching to get back at it.

My thoughts kept returning to the pain I had felt after my dad had passed and I began to feel angry again at everyone and everything. I somehow felt that running each day provided me an outlet for these negative feelings and often a way to connect with my dad. I craved running.

It was then that I came up with the idea to run every day. When we landed I looked at Traci and told her something that would sound crazy to most. I told her I was going to run the next 923 days in a row for my dad.

I wanted to run 923 days in a row to symbolize the day T passed away: September 23. When he passed, a part of me passed with him and I saw this as a way to reconnect.

I could see by her expression she was concerned. She knew from experience that when I put my mind to something I always accomplished it, but she was worried I might hurt myself or break down if somehow life got in my way of making sure I ran every single day.

I understood her concern, but it didn't stop me. She told me she would support me and I knew my dad would be proud of this new challenge I was about to take. I wanted to create a legacy that I could share with my dad and this was going to be it. When Traci started asking me the details of my new plan, I told her my goal was to run at least four miles a day for the next 923 days. I would run whether I was healthy or sick. If an injury plagued me, I would find a way to run through it. If I was tired, I wouldn't use it as an excuse. Nothing was going to hold me back.

Like any great master plan, this one had to have some rules. Traci helped me create the rules that day on the tarmac and for the first year of my running streak, only the two of us knew about them.

The rules were pretty simple and unlike most of the running streaks I had ever read about. Most streaks require runners to put in one mile per day. I read stories about people who kept their streak alive by running down airplane concourses, up and down hospital stairs or just around the block, but I set out with a more stringent plan in mind.

After about a year of running every day and following my rules, people began to notice my weight loss and lack of rest days. They started asking what I was doing, so eventually I shared the rules with others.

The Rules of the Streak

1. My runs could only take place on a treadmill, track, trail, or road; nothing else would count. I threw the treadmill in just in case I got into real trouble somewhere and had to run a quick four miles. The reason I chose four miles was that when I started running the Gateway Loop in the McDowell Mountains it was just over four miles. I knew I could always escape to run a quick loop out there as I had done so many times before.
2. All four miles must be run. Walking would not count towards the streak.
3. If I was in the middle of a night race and it happened to extend into the next morning, the only miles that would count would be the ones that I ran. This rule primarily applied to ultra-running because so often at the end of a race you're subjected to walking to the finish line. (This was a later addition to the rules because at the time the rules were made I had no idea what an ultra-marathon was and I did all my running in the morning.)
4. I allowed myself the entire day to complete the miles. Some streaks require no more than 24 hours in between runs and while 95 percent of mine followed suit, I left this rule open in case traveling caused us to travel into a different time zone, complicating things. I would have several of those days during the streak where I would start late at night and run all night and into the next

> morning to maximize my time off. I figured if I ran Thursday morning early and then not again until Friday at 11 pm, I would have almost a day and a half off, saving my legs in case they were too tired.

I did worry a little about how I was going to handle my new plan once the summer arrived. I figured I would need to endure three Arizona summers in order to finish this streak, but spending at least 30 minutes or four miles a day with my thoughts (which usually gravitated toward T) would be worth the dreadful 100-degree weather.

At that point I had never run a race farther than a 5K and I was starting to get the itch. Before I would commit to a race, I needed to learn more. I had envisioned running some 5K or 10K trail races but there was no part of me that ever thought I would run a marathon, let alone an ultra-marathon. In fact, I had never heard of an ultra-marathon when I started the streak. I was never worried about injury from running too fast or too far. I figured if I ran my token four miles every day, I would stay healthy, keep my weight down, and my mental state would stay strong.

Chapter 8: Who Are These People That Run Ultras?

On Memorial Day weekend 2010, I got a text from my wife's friend Ed Wagner, saying that he and his training partner Deb Hamberlin were coming to the McDowell Mountains to do a 13-mile loop. I was welcome to join them if I wanted. I was terrified. Never in my life had I run more than five miles and even though I was running the Gateway Loop every day, I still had not pushed myself. After debating back and forth in my mind all evening I finally decided to give it a go. Part of me asked, "How much harder can 13 miles be? I can already run five."

I met Ed and Deb at the trailhead. I was immediately freaked out by the trails we were about to tackle. While the McDowell Mountains are basically in my back yard, there are 50 miles of trails I had never explored. Maybe it was out of fear or maybe it had something to do with my poor navigational skills that I had never ventured onto new trails.

That morning we ran that loop in a few hours. We talked and talked and before I knew it I had completed a half-marathon of trails! Not just any half-marathon; we ran up Bell Pass, over East End, up Tom's Thumb and down. This route entailed 3,800 feet of climbing and a big push out of my previous comfort zone of 1,000 feet of climbing.

During the run we talked about their training, why they run so far, and what races they were training for. They talked at length about an upcoming race called the Javelina Jundred. They planned to run the race together with the goal of just finishing. They didn't have any time goals but wanted to finish in less than 30 hours, the course cutoff.

I listened to the conversation and asked the occasional question, but really the same thoughts kept entering my head: Who in their right mind would ever want to run 100 miles, and was this really possible? They didn't look like super humans. I wondered why, if these races are happening all over the world, had I never heard of them? I watched the news and followed sports and never once had I heard someone mention the phrase ultra-marathon. I began to think it was a made-up sport for a group of underground runners who didn't like pounding the pavement of a marathon. I asked how many days it would take, and how would they carry food, tents, water, and lights? They looked at me and said they would run it in one day, or one day and a couple of hours. Sure, you run 100 miles in 24 hours, I thought, there is absolutely no way this was possible.

Not wanting to offend these new friends, I held my laughter and skepticism to myself. When I got home I told Traci that Ed and Deb might be crazy because they thought they were going to run 100 miles in one day. Traci mentioned that Ed had talked about the race with her before but she had never really given it a second thought. I immediately did what we all do when we're looking for information—I Googled it.

On the Internet I found that these types of runners are called ultra-runners. The more I read, the more I was intrigued by the idea of running crazy distances in the mountains or cross-country.

The next two days, I went out and ran the same 13-mile loop by myself and was hooked. I wasn't just hooked on running; I was intrigued by the distance. I wanted to be an ultra-runner.

So many thoughts went through my mind: What does one possibly think about for 24 to 30 hours while only running? How much weight do you lose? What do you eat? You do eat, right? Do a lot of people die from running ultra-marathons? Are they sanctioned?

When I wasn't working or running, I spent the evenings reading and learning just how people accomplished these crazy ultra-marathon distances. I surmised that an ultra-runner's toughest competition did not come from the other runners on the course, but from the mind and body. Although I didn't think I was going to be able to go right out and run a 100-mile race I did want to start running shorter ultra trail races and work my way up. I thought, "I can do this, I've been battling with my own mind for a while now, so might be this is exactly the kind of race where I would excel."

Chapter 9: A Full Moon and Trails Await

By September of 2010, Deb and Ed convinced me to run in my first ultra-marathon which was a 12-hour night run at the Pemberton Trail in Fountain Hills, Arizona. This happened to be the same location where the Javelina Jundred would be run just one month later.

The Pemberton Trail is a 15.4-mile loop that is relatively flat with aid stations every 7.5 miles. The object of the race was to run as many laps as one could in 12 hours, or just run a loop or two if that was all that was desired. There were about 200 runners signed up that evening and in talking with people it seemed as though most people were just going to run one loop and go home. Of course there were those few trying to run three or four loops. The only rules were that you couldn't start any loops after 3 am and the mileage only counted for full, completed loops.

I went into the race telling Traci I would run one and if I felt okay I would run a second. The longest I had ever run going into this race was 22 miles. In order to go farther than that in this race, I would have to extend it to close to 31 miles so I kept my expectations low.

About a week before the race we were at our friend Tere's house discussing this race. After hearing about it, she said she would run some of the race with me if I wanted. I wasn't sure what the rules of the race were since it was more of a fun run than a competition, but when I looked, you were allowed to have a pacer if you were running farther than two loops. When we started dinner I told her I only planned on running one loop because I had never run more than 22 miles and she quickly told me that if I could run a 22-mile training run, I would have no issue finishing 31 miles in a race. She explained that the endorphins kick in and when you're in competition the miles fly by much faster than during a training run.

To me everything she said seemed very logical and even Traci said that I should at least try to run two loops. If I finished two loops, I would have completed my first ultra-marathon. While completing an ultra-marathon was never on my bucket list, I did like the sound of having a medal for my accomplishment. At the time I wasn't sure if this was as far as I would ever go or if this was the start of bigger things.

As the night continued and we had a couple drinks, I started to ask Tere and Traci what they thought about me trying to go three laps. If I went three laps, my entire third loop could be completed with a pacer. With someone talking to me and encouraging me while I ran, I figured it would be pretty easy. I'm not sure I was completely sold on running 46.2 miles but Tere and Traci were 100 percent behind me so in my mind I decided if others didn't see failure as an option, neither could I. The worst thing that could happen was I would have to drop out of the race early and Tere wouldn't get the chance to pace me.

By the time the conversation finished I had decided I was running three loops, 46.2 miles, and had arranged for Tere to meet me at midnight to pace the last 15.4 miles. Traci had confidence I would finish and meet my goal; I, on the other hand, wasn't so sure. This was going to be 24 miles farther than any run I had ever attempted and I would be running this race throughout the night under the full moon.

The Javelina Night run at Pemberton crept up on me much quicker than I had anticipated and while I felt semi-ready for the race I wasn't sure how I was going to do with my new goal of running 46.2 miles. I had never run a race farther than a 5K (3.1 miles) but was setting out to complete 75K. What was I thinking?

I had been training for the 25K (15.4 miles) trail race and somehow I had managed to talk myself into running 75K (46.2 miles).The first week of October in 2010 would be show time and I was starting to get scared to death.

I normally do not schedule anything on Saturdays in the fall besides Michigan football, but since they had an afternoon game, I would have plenty of time to watch the Michigan game. I also thought if they won, it would improve my mental state and I would be able to use that as encouragement or a happy thought during the low moments on the course. I couldn't find any reason why I wouldn't finish the race as long I maintained a positive attitude and had fun. There is a lot to be said about having fun while racing instead of making it seem like a job.

Refusing to succumb to the excuses in my head, I began the 46.2-mile race at 6 pm Saturday night with the goal of finishing the three 25K loops by 6 am the next day. In my mind, I was going to finish this race even if I had to walk the entire way. I don't like to make a goal and fall short and there was no way I was going to let this day be any different.

As 200 runners all stood around the starting line, nervous energy ran through my veins like ice water. I was restless and ready to get started. I couldn't believe I had signed up for an ultra-marathon before I even thought about running a marathon. I kept thinking the next 12 hours were not going to end well, but Traci assured me I would be fine. She also reminded me that if I ran into trouble, there would be plenty of places to stop and try again another day.

I was attempting a run that was 24 miles farther than I had ever completed on a training run and frankly I was pretty freaked out at the unknown. Then again, I had also made the spur of the moment decision to do three 25K loops just days before, so I could blame no one but myself if it ended poorly. I thought maybe I needed to take a few steps back and check my ego at the door and try to complete two loops, not three. Most ultra-runners have very little ego because this is not a sport where winning reaps any bigger reward than one would get for simply finishing a 5K. Yet the thrill of competition is tough to deny, even for the most laid-back runner.

At 6pm we took off into McDowell Mountain Park in the hot 100-degree Arizona sun. As the sun began to set a little over the mountains, I began to feel the confidence I had hoped for going into the day. My goal was to run each loop with my friends Ed and Deb and even though they were more prepared for a race like this, I thought if I could just keep my legs moving, it would be enough to stay with them for the whole night. Since my goal was three evenly paced loops, I would set out to stay with them unless they sped up and tried to run out of my comfort zone. They had a goal of running four loops, as they were training for the Javelina Jundred the next month. They told me they would try to run four three-hour loops all the way through, and they again reminded me that speed was my only enemy. Ultra-running is only about speed if your plan is to win a race. As for rest of us, the only thing that matters is the satisfaction of crossing the finish line in one piece.

We traversed the sandy trails through the Sonoran Desert and chatted away as we made our way up the small rocky hill that eventually leveled out to a virtually flat loop called the Pemberton trail. This trail has some small rolling hills, but no major climbs you would see in some of the bigger ultra-races.

Rolling hill by rolling hill we made our way around the course and the three of us stayed together and discussed everything from my transformation into a runner to what Deb was planning for dinner the next week all the way into the finish of the first loop.

Being my first ultra, I wasn't really prepared with the best food choices. I had never tried a synthetic food source for calories such as GU or gel. These little 100-calorie sticky packets seemed to be the choice of most runners but I had no idea whether they would agree with my stomach or not, so I avoided them and stuck with a few items off the aid station buffet. They had potato chips, pretzels, pumpkin pie, water, melon, vegan items, soda, and electrolyte drinks, none matching my stomach's lack of appetite. Yet I knew calories were necessary if I was going to continue on with the race. I grabbed a few pretzels, which tasted so dry I could barely swallow. This might have provided me 100 calories if I was lucky. My friends had packed peanut butter and jelly squares and were munching on those as we left the aid station.

I think it was the time of day and the lack of calories in my system that left me tired and sluggish as we continued on. We made our way up the never-ending six-mile climb and with no real food to contend with, I could feel what was only liquid sloshing around in my stomach. At this point, I began to worry about my future in the race. I had some snacks in my backpack that Deb encouraged me to eat, but I still worried about getting sick. I decided it would be okay to take down a pack of the jelly beans I had brought and almost instantly felt relieved.

I quickly learned that your mood and physical feelings can change quickly in a run like this. While I began to feel a boost of energy, Ed began to get sick. He told Deb and me to go ahead. We planned to meet up with him again at the next aid station. Ed must have been struggling because it was too long of a wait to stay at the next station so Deb and I pushed on without him.

Deb and I arrived at the midway aid station and she told me to go ahead while she used the bathroom and picked up some extra food from the aid station. I walked out of the aid station, hoping Deb would catch me in a few minutes, but I never saw her headlight coming up from behind me. I was pretty devastated because there were 8.5 miles left in the second loop and I worried I wouldn't know what to do if I got into trouble out on the trail. I was still so new to this whole trail running thing, and running my first race in the middle of the night with the coyotes howling wasn't helping my anxiety.

After a few minutes of waiting, I decided I might as well start to run again because I had a pacer waiting for me to begin the third loop. Looking down at my Garmin watch, I noticed that I was just about to cross the 22-mile mark, which was farther than I had ever gone before. I wanted so badly to have someone to celebrate with but there was absolutely no one around. How was it possible that I was running with 200 other runners, switching directions on each loop, and it appeared there was no one for a mile in either direction? When my watch beeped I broke down into tears and pointed to the sky just as I did every morning in the McDowell Mountains talking to T. Instead of a quiet conversation with him, I yelled "I did it, that's for you Dad." I couldn't have been more excited. I was reminded again that in ultra-running, the highest of highs can trigger the lowest of lows.

Within a matter of minutes, I went from feeling on top of the world to feeling so ill I could barely stand up. The lack of calories was killing me and I was beginning to sway from side to side as if I was drunk. I finally had to sit down in the desert. It wasn't that I felt nauseous; it was more like I had the flu. My whole body felt as though it was shutting down and there was nothing I could do about it.

Sitting down, my mind began to wander out of the present to how would I finish the race? Better yet, how was I going to finish this loop? Better yet, how was I going to finish the loop and start a third? I had zero energy and nothing in my bag seemed to taste good, fueling my anxiety. Finally I found some orange jelly beans buried in the bottom of my bag. These jelly beans were like tiny morsels of heaven. I grabbed my cell phone out of my bag and told Traci I was taking a few moments to gather myself, but expected to finish my second loop around midnight. "Please make sure Tere is there to pace me."

As I sat on the ground in the middle of the desert, talking to her on my cell phone, my sheer exhaustion caused me to ramble. Traci later told me I sounded like I was drunk. I'm sure being drunk would have been a much better feeling than what I was going through. I was just running on empty and could barely function. She asked what I wanted her to get ready and have available when I got to the next aid station. The only thought that came to my mind was that I wanted things that were orange. There was a long pause on the other line and then Traci said "What?" I said I wanted oranges, orange Gatorade, orange candy, whatever you can come up with that is orange in color. I felt like I was having a pregnancy craving but that was all I wanted. It was an odd feeling for the next few miles, as all I thought about were things that were orange. I tried to make lists in my head of things that were orange and thought about how good they would taste going into my stomach. I was having dreams about Orange Crush soda and jumping orange jellybeans for some crazy reason. Was I delirious? Whatever it was, the pack of orange jellybeans I took down had removed the sloshing from my stomach and left me feeling like I could get moving again at a moderate pace.

I knew I wasn't going to be running as fast as I had in the first lap, but at least I wasn't about to tip over. I was moving down the trail with a purpose.

I finished my second loop at 11:50 pm. I came into the aid station hooting and hollering. Because I crossed the time line with 10 minutes to go, it meant I could start a third loop with a pacer if I chose to. Traci handed me more orange items than I even knew existed. I chomped down on a few items, threw some in my bag, and Tere and I headed out for my final loop. Running the third loop with a pacer provided me a sense of security. She would keep an eye on me and make sure I didn't fall over and die in the middle of the desert. This was going to be a fun loop, and not only was every step I took a new personal record for distance, I was about to learn more about myself than I had ever imagined.

The body is tough, and often the mind is weak, but in order to complete an ultra, you must possess a strong mind. You must also have patience. Not only was I lucky to pick up a pacer for loop three, but my pacer just so happened to be a sports psychologist. For miles she spoke of positive thoughts and ways to overcome the mind.

Before I knew it, miles were passing by and my goal of 46.2 miles was getting closer and closer. I was doing great and running well until a runner on his second lap approached at mile 38. I asked him how far to the aid station and he said about 1.25 miles. I thought, "Okay, I will pick up the pace, get to the aid station, hydrate, and then finish up the last 7.5 miles." Not quite how it went since I wasted all my energy and water trying to get to the aid station. Rather than quickly refueling and getting back out to finish the race, I started to get extremely dizzy as I arrived at the aid station. My head began to spin. I felt as though I was having an out-of-body experience where I could see people talking around me, but couldn't hear or comprehend their mumble. I thought I was done, but the image of a "Did Not Finish" next to my name after all that I had already gone through was not something I was willing to accept.

Quick on her feet, Tere wrangled up some oranges, water, and salt tablets. I managed to pull my body off the ground and get up and shuffle my feet for the last 7.5 miles.

I ran like I have never run before and the pain never seemed to cross my mind. We worked well as a team and as I approached the final road crossing with a sign reading 1.5 miles to the finish I looked at Tere and said "Let's go!" I had spent enough time out on the course and while my body was exhausted, my mind had overcome a lot and it was strong. I was ready for a big finish. I crossed the finish line in ninth place out of 183 finishers.

The thrill of finishing was like nothing I've experienced. Only three people would go on to run the full 100K and there were only five faster times in the 75K. In the days that followed, I kept thinking of how amazing it felt to complete such a challenge.

When I was young, I was told by doctors that I might never be able to walk straight, let alone run. At one point I feared never being able to play sports, and now I had just run 46 miles in a row!

Chapter 10: Learning to Walk

When I turned three, my parents took me to the doctor for what they thought was going to be a routine physical examination. I received my yearly shots and the doctor took my height and weight. Then when he asked if my parents had any questions, they voiced a concern to him about the way I walked. The doctor observed me walking across the office a few times and then told me parents that he would like to run a few tests because he wasn't sure why I was walking pigeon toed. I was struggling to make routine movements with my legs, so he referred me to a specialist who could take a look at my growth development and to try and figure out why I was walking this way.

My parents were told that I had a genetic disorder that had resulted in deformed shin bones. While I was too young to understand the gravity of what the specialists were saying, my parents were worried that I might never walk straight. My legs were wobbly at best and the only way for me to improve, the doctor said, was to wear cables on my legs. I would need to wear them for a few years in hopes that this would straighten them out. My parents wanted a quicker fix so I wouldn't have to go through this. They asked if surgery was an option, but were told it was not. I was stuck with cables.

Every month I would go in and see the doctors and they would make adjustments to tighten up the cables. This was similar to how kids go in to orthodontists today to get their braces adjusted. My age freed me from worrying about these cables; I actually liked having these cables on my legs. In fact, my parents would even tell stories of how I insisted on wearing the braces outside of my pants instead of inside like everyone else because I wasn't embarrassed or ashamed of my condition. For some reason I wanted to let people know I had cables on my legs.

Times were different than they are today. Back then, no one would have said anything negative to me about the cables. The movie Forrest Gump hadn't even come out. If I had worn the cables after the movie hit the big screens, I'm sure I would have been made fun of or called Forrest my whole life, but back then my friends seemed to think it was normal. For months the doctors said my legs were getting a little better, which was great news. However, they insisted I wear the cables for at least another year if I expected to see positive results. My parents were told that if the cables didn't work over the course of a couple years I might never walk upright. This also meant I wouldn't be able to play any sports.

My parents remained positive and took me to the doctor constantly to make sure the cables were doing their job. After a year and a half the doctors delivered the exceptional news that my legs had improved dramatically and I could finally take the cables off for good. My parents remained a little nervous that with the cables off, the condition might show up again later in life. However, the doctors assured them that I would be able to run, play sports, and live a normal everyday life like the rest of my friends, now that my legs had straightened out. Finally, I was going to be able to do activities that I had held me back in the past. No longer would I be visiting the doctor monthly to get the cables tightened. Maybe best of all, I could play sports!

***

Our family grew up in a good neighborhood full of kids our age. There was never a moment that my brother Bryan and I weren't outside playing sports. When we each turned five, our mom and dad signed us up for soccer. Soccer had a positive influence on my life because it was the first opportunity I had with my dad as the coach of one of my teams.

T didn't know much about the game of soccer prior to starting the season but there was no doubt in our minds that he would make a good coach. He teamed up with a family friend, Mick, from down the street and they began to study the game. He read books on soccer and watched other teams practice. He really started to understand how the game should be played and developed a plan to make our team the best in the league.

See, our team was built on speed while most other teams in the league were all about the skills. We were small and undersized like most kids were but we moved with precision across the field. Since T recognized that the kids on our team were quick, we worked on running drills to get even faster. Most teams didn't work on running drills at this age so we created a competitive advantage. Our goal was to spread out on the field so the defense would get tired from covering us and running up and down the field so many times.

T's plan worked! We won the season and it didn't take me very long to buy into my T's coaching methods. It was then that I learned that hard work pays off.

When it wasn't soccer season, my dad would join my friends and me in neighborhood baseball games. My friends would always tell me how cool they thought it was that he would come out and play. I think T knew that some of the other kids had parents who never made time for their children, so he would patiently listen to their stories even when they were about the wildest things. He always appeared interested no matter how boring I thought the stories were.

T gained a lot of respect from my friends back then. When we all became teenagers it was evident how much they appreciated him, continuing to show him every bit of respect. It was admirable. When he was done playing catch, he would go inside and play house or school with my sister Jill. He never wanted to miss any part of our childhood.

We ate dinner as a family on most nights and the five of us would talk about everything. Most kids are reluctant or uninterested in sharing what went on in their day, but since we often talked about sports we never sat around a quiet dinner table.

Chapter 11: Cave Creek Thriller 50K

Just weeks after running the Javelina Night Run, I decided it was time to see how I compared with some of the other local ultra-runners. I really had no idea what to expect or how hard the race was going to be, but I signed up for the Cave Creek Thriller 50K.

This was the first race in a new trail series by Aravaipa Running called the Desert Runners Trail Series. I knew a bunch of local runners would be registering and I wanted to see how I would match up. This course consisted of five 6.5-mile loops, each with over 1,000 feet of elevation gain. While I wasn't particularly fond of another looped course, I was confident I could hold my own if I focused on proper nutrition and refueling throughout the day.

When the other runners showed up at the start of the race on race morning, I looked each over, sizing up my competition. I felt like there were some great runners in the field but I got super nervous when I saw Michael Miller show up in race gear.

Michael Miller was an experienced ultra-runner who had just run the Javelina Jundred in 19.5 hours a week prior. He ranked within the top 2 percent of the sport. He was in his late 40s and as fit of a runner as you will ever find. He showed up at the starting line with no shirt and these funny-looking clown shoes on his feet. It was tough for me to look at those things on his feet and not think I was racing some European running sensation. I mean who else wore these shoes? I had never seen them in any store before but then again I was still relatively new to the sport.

We exchanged pleasantries at the start line but my nerves were starting to get the best of me and I probably didn't make any sense while he tried to make conversation with me. I imagined him to be an emotionless runner who dominated the local ultra-running scene.

I figured Michael would lead the pack from the start, but he humbly spoke before the start to say, "This old man will be going slow today, I just ran 100 miles last weekend." In my mind I thought, how in the world can this guy stand after running 100 miles, let alone run another 50K? Couldn't he just give us newbies a break and sit this race out so we had a chance? He carried just one water bottle in his hands and a sweat towel, but when he saw my camelback hydration pack he jokingly said, "Real men carry their bottles; my wife carries a pack." Who did this guy think he was? The race had not even begun and he was already getting in my head.

We took off and headed down the short asphalt road toward the trail for the first climb. Right away I felt a letdown coming on. My breathing was erratic, I started out way too fast and I was the second person heading up the hill. To my surprise, the lead runner was not Michael Miller, but rather another runner who looked like a mountain goat as he made his way up to the summit. I tried to keep pace, but for every step I took forward, he seemed to get two steps ahead of me.

Part of me was ready to throw in the towel and settle for a back-of-the-pack finish. I began to think I was just not as good as most of the people who had been running ultras for years; but then we approached the downhill.

Running downhill has always been my favorite part of running trails and I hold it in high regard since the first mile I ever ran was in the rocky downhill terrain in the McDowell Mountains. Unlike many, I never worry about the rocky terrain and I thrive on slippery gravel slopes. Many people talk about how much they hate steep descents, but this is an area I excel in. I practiced running hard downhill every day in the McDowell's, trying to beat my time from the day before, and while it often puts cuts on my knees and palms, it never discourages me from going fast.

I took off at a reckless speed down the first hill. As we made our way to the start line for the second loop, I had the lead runner in sight. There was no one behind me for at least a mile. I rolled into the aid station where Traci refilled my hydration pack right on my back and sent me off for lap two. Before leaving the aid station, many people yelled that the lead runner was close and I could get him if I pushed it. I really didn't see any need to push the pace this early in the race and could tell from the first loop that he was a better climber than I. But I was a better downhill runner.

When you can run fast downhill, you can make up a lot of time on a runner who is moving gingerly down the rough terrain. Within minutes, I could see him at the top of the hill. I was struggling to run a 12-minute pace up the hill, but my confidence had returned and my legs felt good. I told myself to run nice and easy and wait to hammer the downhill section. I would have five opportunities to do this throughout the race, so if I could keep him within sight, I might be able to overtake him later in the race.

I battled through the next two loops the same as the first two, keeping the lead runner within sight. Then, at mile 22, I started to feel excruciating pain in my legs and baseball-size bulges were coming out the backs of my calves. Being relatively new to the sport, I had no idea what to do about this issue. Having heard about salt tablets, I carried some just in case, but I really had no idea what they were for. I figured now was the time, so I popped a few, only to find they were no magic remedy.

I sat down on a hard, sharp rock, calves bulging, and rubbed my legs to ease the pain. The pain just seemed to get worse. I saw shirtless Michael Miller quickly approaching from behind and decided I had to get up or I was going to finish this race third. I tried and barely made it a few steps before I was sitting down again, yelling obscenities at the rocks. I looked back again and Michael drew even closer, so I decided to suck it up and slog my way to the downhill and hope that running the mile back to the start line would loosen up my legs. My legs were tight and the stabbing feeling in my calves was getting worse. I had no choice but to get moving or get passed. I knew if I got passed, it would be a huge mental setback for me, so I worked through the pain and began to walk it off.

Within moments I began to feel okay again and the cramps started to fade. I don't know if it was the effect of the salt tablets or if I was able to switch my brain off and accept the pain. Regardless, I ran down the final hill to finish the fourth lap. As I did, I saw the leader still at the aid station.

He also had come into a little bit of trouble and the heat was starting to wear on him. He looked back and saw me and started to worry about his lead for the first time all day. I could see him pouring ice-cold water over his head with a sponge before he quickly took off up the hill. He knew he needed to put a little bit of a gap between us or I was going to have a chance to catch him when we got to the downhill section. I made my way into the aid station, quickly refilled my bag and headed out. I wasn't able to run the hill because my legs wobbled like a fresh Jell-O mold, but I put my hands on my knees and power-hiked up the hill. This was probably the fastest I had moved all day and about 200 yards before the top I finally overtook the leader with just five miles to go in the race. My heart was pounding. He had led for the first 26 miles and when he saw me pass, it was clear it affected his psyche. In true trail-runner style, he praised my effort and told me to finish strong. He wasn't worried that his race was over, but was happy I was still moving well after a day of chasing him.

During the final lap, I found myself looking back every few minutes to see if he was going to regain steam. After the first climb, I couldn't see him. I took my time as we wound our way around the back of the mountain but the 90-plus degree heat was really beginning to take its toll on me. I was just about out of water as I hit the final aid station, which was only two miles from the finish. Then as I was filling up my pack, I heard the volunteers start to yell "Yay Miller!" Holy shit! This guy had come out of absolutely nowhere and was within two minutes of me. I wasn't moving fast, but I wasn't dragging either. I had absolutely no idea how he could have made up so much ground. Michael had run even splits every loop, leaving him to contend for the win during the final lap.

After leaving the final aid station, I started to prepare my mind for the last two miles. We would have a one-mile climb before the final descent. What I did not know how to plan for was Michael. Since I had not had a chance to see him race all day I wasn't sure how his body or mind was holding up. Every time I turned around to see how he looked, it seemed like he was doing great. He was running strong and looked the same as when we had started the race.

While Michael looked cool, calm and collected, I was anything but calm. I wasn't happy at all with myself, nor with him. Who was this guy to rain on my one chance of winning an ultra? This was my first 50K. How cool would it be to win my first-ever 50K? Heading up the hill Michael continued to shorten the gap between us. Unsure of his race-closing abilities, I assumed I would have to race all the way to the finish, ending with a photo finish between the two of us.

I really didn't know if my legs had it in them to race. Was this guy with the clown shoes and bare chest all of a sudden going to take off and leave me in the dust? I had to get out of my head or I would surely lose the race. I was struggling to have anything but negative thoughts as we made our way to the top of the climb. I finally looked up, pointed to my dad and told him I was going to win this race for him.

My eyes began to well with tears. The thought of winning my first-ever 50K was a little overwhelming but it was far from over. I took one last look back and decided it was time to give it everything I had for the last mile, even if I would pass out at the finish line. I was never known for my speed as a child, but I finished that last mile in a six-minute pace and took the win by over three minutes!

As I lay sprawled out on the ground after the race, Michael and his wife walked over to me. He congratulated me on my win. The man I thought was an elite runner with an ego turned out to be the typical representative of the trail-running community. He didn't have an ego and, in fact, was one of the nicest people I had ever met. He could not have cared less about losing the race; he was there to celebrate a new trail series with his wife and have some fun out on the trails. We talked for nearly 20 minutes about how cool the trail-running community was and he expressed how I would be a great fit on the Arizona ultra-scene. Really? Was he talking about me or was he just being nice? He wasn't just being nice; he was being himself. Michael Miller represents exactly what every trail-runner should aspire to be. He is a kind, caring person who cares more about the people running than any race result.

My victory in this race felt like a personal victory as well. It was my first win and my first clear sign that I was beginning to take control of my life. I determined the outcome and I decided whether I was going to let negative thoughts take me over in the final minutes of the race, or choose to conjure up positive ones that would propel me forward. I had found a passion in running that healed my soul every day. Yet, in a mental game of putting the cart before the horse, I wondered: Would I have ever found this passion for running if it weren't for the grief I experienced after losing T?

Chapter 12: Family Life

My dad was a family man who spent every moment making sure that my mom, my brother, my sister and I were properly cared for. He was never one who bought expensive things for himself or drove a fancy car. His first priority was fulfilling the needs of his family. I always felt that no matter what I did my dad would be there to love and support me. I loved how he never judged me when I made big mistakes. When others shared negative opinions about me or my future he stood up for me. He believed in me and made me believe in myself.

It was clear to me that T had lots of friends and co-workers who thought highly of him. Every time one of his friends would introduce themselves to me or my brother, they would say something incredible about him. Bryan and I felt like we were with royalty when we were with him at Michigan football games and it wasn't that he demanded respect; he received respect because of the genuine person he was. He would ask everyone about their families and get to know his employees on a personal level. The younger workers thought of him as a father figure that they could go to for advice. He had been a fixture at his company since he finished college at the age of 22.

In today's world, most of us will change careers seven times in a lifetime, but T was a loyal man and loved his company that had taken a chance on him. Loyalty is one of the traits I admire most about my father.

He worked for the same company for 35 years and I never heard him say a negative comment about that company, even when they let him go. I felt the pain in my dad's voice when he told me he was let go from his job. Being the optimist he was, he forced a smile and told me it would be okay.

Anxiety has always been a big problem for me and hearing my dad say "I lost my job today" really made me worry. How could a company let a man go who has put his heart and soul into a job for 35 years? His early departure from there made me worry about my job and really made me question whether one should ever be loyal to their employer. My dad continued to reaffirm his decision to stay loyal and carefully explained to me that sometimes it is in the best interest of a business to go another direction.

I feared for my dad's livelihood; would they have enough money to live on? Would my mom have to go back to work? At the time I lived far away and thought of all those times he helped me when I was down, and that I wasn't there as a shoulder for him to lean on. Every night when I would pick up the phone to call him on my way home from work, I worried that he might be upset or depressed, but he never dwelled on the situation.

After nine months my dad reentered the employment market for a similar company in his industry. I could tell from the day he started it wasn't the best fit for him and his heart was still with his former company. He had worked so hard to make his former company one of the leaders in their industry and now he was working for a competitor. I could always tell from the inflection of his voice that he didn't feel right working for them but he was still a few years from retirement.

The realization that he wasn't meant to be at this new company hit him about the same time it hit his former employer that they were struggling without him on staff. His former co-workers and superiors missed the man who brought more than just intelligence to the table. He was a man of honor, a man of his word. He never looked for a way to pass the buck but instead stood up and faced the criticisms and found answers. He had been away for three years when a call came in from his former employer that they would like to speak with him. My dad had been hearing from co-workers at his former company that they were looking to bring him back on staff. He graciously accepted the offer to come back and work for them and he continued just as he had that fateful day he started 35 years prior.

***

My parents instilled in us early on that schoolwork was just as important as our ability to get better at different sports. Each night we would sit around the kitchen table to finish homework.

This is where T and I did not see eye to eye. He had a love for mathematics and while I was good at it I really wasn't that interested in spending the time doing the work. I wanted to be outside playing basketball or at the batting cage hitting, but I didn't get much of a choice. It was during a geometry session that I would try and tell T the stuff they were trying to teach us was useless and I would never use it in my life. I mean, who cares how you figure out the area of a triangle or the different amount of material needed to fill a certain space? We would have battles there at the table about the importance of learning this material. Usually they would end with me spouting off some disrespectful, "I don't care." But he would never get mad.

It made me so mad that he wouldn't just explode back at me and send me to my room. It just wasn't how he was. These one-sided screaming matches would stress my mom out, but it was his calm nature that eventually made me understand that I was going to have to learn this stuff if I ever expected to move on in school. This was a required class and no matter how much I didn't like the thought of learning about it, the reality was I would be stuck in the ninth grade forever if I didn't take the time to figure it out.

T never had a mean bone in his body. He always had the ability to step back from an explosive situation and make it better.

If there was a magic pill that I could take to calm me down and put me in the moment just as T always was I would have cartons upon cartons of those suckers never farther than a hand's reach away. Instead, I was "gifted" with the gene of anxiety. I know there is medicine out there that can help with anxiety, but sometimes what works best for me when I get super-impatient is remembering the words my dad would say to me back when I struggled through that lousy homework. "Patience is a virtue and if you use it, good things will come." I hoped that through patience and hard work in my training I would continue to see good results in my races.

Chapter 13: Developing a Community

On Christmas Eve of 2010 I went on a long run with a local Phoenix running group called the Wednesday Morning Running Club. It showed me exactly what makes the trail-running community so special and what a tight-knit family we all are. While I always said I just liked to run for fun, this group showed me how to have a good time out on a run and what trail-running is truly about.

We navigated for three hours through the Phoenix Mountain Preserve. Even though we were climbing all kinds of crazy hills and running through extremely rocky terrain, the smile never wore off my face. Listening to the various people of the group talk and share their stories left me star-struck. I was running with some of the most respected and amazing ultra-runners in the country. Hundred-mile finishers and hundred-mile winners seemed to be the norm in this group. While they spoke of many races while we ran, two particular ones caught my attention. The Old Pueblo 50 Mile down in Sonoita, Ariz. and Zane Grey 50 in Pine, Ariz. really intrigued me.

Old Pueblo seemed to be a great starting race for someone looking to run 50 miles; residing 60 miles south of Tucson, I knew the weather would be in the 60s on race day. To me this meant perfect running conditions.

It didn't take me long after that Christmas Eve run to go home and look up the two races online. At that point 46.2 miles was still my longest-ever distance, but running a few extra miles didn't scare me.

In addition, both races rewarded finishers with either a belt buckle or a finisher's jacket. The famous belt buckle that is usually only associated with 100Ks and 100-mile races was being offered as a finisher's prize at Old Pueblo 50 Mile Endurance Run. I wasn't looking to accessorize, or show off a buckle or jacket, but it would nice to display one as a reminder of the personal strides I had made. I mentally made room for the buckle on my living room bookshelf and cleared any negative thoughts that would keep me from earning my first 50-mile buckle and finish.

***

I had been getting better each and every day that I was running but I did worry about the stress I was putting on my body. I really had no idea how to build a schedule correctly and nothing I could find online really worked with the type of mileage I was putting in. I had thought about looking for a coach in the past but they all seemed to be rather expensive and running was supposed to be for fun, so I wasn't quite sure how to proceed.

My friend Tere had been asking me to come to the track and talk to her coach, John. She thought he was a guy who could really help me out and even though everyone that he coached was a marathon runner, he did have some experience in running ultras in the past.

I was reluctant to ever set foot on a track. I often referred to it as an "oval torture chamber" because I didn't think track practice had any place in ultra-running. However, I was willing to find out what knowledge this coach could share with me and whether or not he would be interested in coaching an ultra-runner.

We talked briefly that evening and when he asked what my goals were I explained my number one goal was to run four miles every day, and secondly I wanted to complete a 50-mile event. As you might expect, he said he wouldn't ever advise anyone to run every day but he did know plenty of people who had also run streaks, and while they had suffered some injuries, there were no more than the average person. He didn't seem concerned by the fact that I said I very much disliked running on the road and would like to run all my miles on trails. I guess I thought this would be a deal breaker for whether or not he would agree to coach me, but it didn't seem to bother him. What was I getting myself into?

John and I sat down and discussed my future as it related to running. I shared with him more details on why I was running and what types of races I might like to enter. I remained vague about my interest in getting any faster. He let me know that he coached a great range of different athletes. Some people he coaches dream of running the Boston Marathon and others just want to run 1,000 meters. I really didn't fit into any of those categories because I wanted to run 50 miles or more, but he assured me that we could outline a schedule that would suit my needs.

Reluctant to buy into his program, at first I made excuses for the few weeks I had a track workout scheduled and I convinced myself I was doing the right thing by avoiding speed work. Everything I had read up to this point always said the fastest way for a runner to get an injury is to run out of their comfort zone. The track was very far out of my comfort zone, and in fact I had never even set foot on one before except to cross over to look at the grass on the football field.

After a few weeks went by, I explained to Traci that I had been purposely missing track workouts because it wasn't something that interested me, and as always she convinced me to give it a try.

That Tuesday afternoon I could feel butterflies floating in my stomach and the anxiety and stress were mounting by the minute. I didn't have track until the evening but I could feel a meltdown coming on. I was anxious about the people on the team, how slow I was, getting hurt, etc., but what ailed me the most was the fear of failure. What if I couldn't complete the workout he had given me? Others would see me quit.

Walking onto the track that Tuesday evening I felt like the kid whose parents decided to move in the middle of the school year, and now I was stuck making all new friends. The runners at the track made the ladies at boot camp look out of shape. These skinny athletes were whipping around the oval with no concerns about the workout times put on their schedule.

Being new to a group certainly has its disadvantages. Often we can only see the negative in situations, and what my mind saw and what was actually in front of me were two different things. My mind said marathon runners were all self-absorbed. I had no factual information to back up these thoughts. I think I felt like they were self-absorbed because none of them talked while they ran. This confused me because I have always been a talker and the rest of the runners were pretty quiet as they made their way around the oval.

What I didn't realize at the time was they were running paces I couldn't even fathom and they were there for one purpose: to put in a hard workout. You can't run that fast and be a chatterbox at the same time.

That evening my coach told me that there would be a few runners that I could do my workout with and we would be doing mile repeats at a 7:30-per-mile pace. By most accounts this is a moderate pace, but for someone who has only run slow miles in ultra-races and training runs, this felt like a sprint. I tried extremely hard to control my mind and focus on the task at hand. Besides, I only had four one-mile repeats; it wasn't like I was going to have to run 50.

While I waited for our coach to tell us to start running, I thought about the fact that I had no idea how to correctly run a loop around the track. I took off at top speed and found myself quickly 25 meters ahead of my group, who seemed to be running comfortably. Round and round we went and when that mile was over, I was hunched over looking for the medical staff. I ran a minute a mile faster than I was supposed to and I had to somehow pick myself off the ground and run three more. I quickly learned the concept of pacing.

For weeks I found myself getting stomach pains every Tuesday afternoon, worrying about how I didn't fit into this group of runners. I thought of myself as an outsider and assumed they looked at me the same way. As quickly as I made up these illusions in my mind, they began to fade as I began to make new friends.

These runners were no different than trail-runners, except they preferred to run on roads. It didn't take long for them to show a genuine interest in the ultra-marathon and for me to similarly engage about races they ran. We both had so many questions, but the one that topped the list was Why? How do you run that far? Does it hurt? Can you walk after running an ultra? I asked the same questions but wondered, How can they run so fast and not get injured?

Chapter 14: Staring Down My First Belt Buckle

Traci and I headed south to Sonoita, Arizona in March of 2011 to tackle my first 50-mile run. I had high expectations for myself for the race. I wasn't thinking about winning, but was fixated on finishing in less than 10 hours. I thought it would be a good starting point for a 50-mile race, especially since I could not foresee any trouble I would get into during the race.

Race morning started off a little chillier than I had anticipated in Sonoita. We pulled up to Kentucky Camp about 5:30 am and I tried to shake the nerves out of my system. My heart was beating a mile a minute and my mind raced, trying to envision exactly what the next nine to 12 hours would be like. To compound my nerves, the temperature at 5,100 feet hovered right around 31 degrees and I was less than prepared to run in colder temperatures.

Traci and I and a couple of friends made our way down the dark quarter-mile hill to the start line. The world seemed silent, with the exception of my heart beating through my chest. Around 5:55 am we toed the starting line, where I turned my headlight on and listened as the race director described the upcoming course. As I stepped up to the start/finish line, drawn in chalk on the ground, I again realized how low-key ultra-running events were in comparison to marathons. I had checked the previous year's results and it appeared that the average finish time was around 11 1/2 hours, which spiked my nerves again as I thought I might have overestimated how quickly I planned on running the course.

My goal for the race was to be between 9.5 and 10 hours. However, I had set this goal before experiencing the Achilles pain that had been plaguing me for the last week. Unsure of whether the pain was a true injury or one of the infamous phantom pains that runners often feel the week before a race, I tried to block it out of my mind.

At about two minutes to 6 am I took one last look down at my watch, said goodbye to my wife as if I was going to war and listened for the start signal. There was no gun, no loud horn; it was the race director counting down, "Three, two, one, go."

Making our way up the pitch-black, dirt forest road at 6 am, I found myself struggling to catch my breath even though we were only at 5,100 feet. For the first quarter-mile I battled the demons in my mind. Maybe I was still dealing with the nervous energy or maybe it was the elevation, but again I could hear my heart beating in my chest as I tried to stay in the second group of runners and ascend the first long climb. I turned up my iPod a little louder to distract me from my own thoughts and so my heartbeat didn't sound so loud and bothersome. I tried to get my mind off the fact that it was going to be a long day.

We reached a parking area and made a left turn that headed down a rolling forest road for a couple of miles. I was in the second group of four runners. I had done my homework going into the race. I spoke to fellow runners who had experience on the course and I attempted to study course maps. I am somewhat directionally challenged and never really feel confident telling the difference between north and south, but I hoped that at least getting a preview of the terrain would help me to prepare for what was in front of me.

The veteran runners warned me not to get stuck behind others on the initial single-track portion of the course that wound through the mountains. I would need to position myself towards the front of the larger group early.

About 1.5 miles in, the four runners ahead of me took off into what appeared to be a sprint for the lead position. My pack backed off because the pace was far too fast for us to maintain, especially this early in the run. I did not envision having to wear myself out in the first two miles of a 50-mile race. I immediately thought about the advice my coach gave me about staying conservative early and not getting too aggressive. He preached running my own race, not getting sucked into someone else's. While I initially thought this was obvious, I soon realized how many runners, including me, struggle with this concept when they start a race.

As the lead group extended their lead I cleared my head and was able to regain a normal breathing pattern as we headed towards the first aid station at mile two. I decided not to stop at the aid station and maintained my pace, now settling in with the second pack of runners.

Just when I thought I had shaken my nerves for the day, I came across my first obstacle. The course was lined with blue-and-white ribbons but it was dark, and even with our headlights on, some of the other runners and I missed a turn that would take us onto the Arizona Trail. I guess checking those maps before the race did me little good as far as navigating the path correctly. It took us about a mile and a half to realize our mistake and turn around. Devastation and anger were my first reactions. I had run 1.5 miles out of my way and now I had to backtrack another 1.5 miles (uphill) to get back on course. I was so mad at myself for making such a dumb mistake, but there were four of us who had turned wrong, so at least my ignorance had company. I regained my composure and figured it was best to stay calm and not overreact.

The good news was that the pack was running at such a good pace, concentrating on each step, that the error didn't cost us that much time. I could hear the frustration in one of the runners and wanted to join in on the pity-party, but I reminded myself it would be an even longer day if negative thoughts overtook me this early. We made our way back up the dirt road and turned onto the Arizona Trail only to find we were the last runners to hit this section of the trail. As I said, it was single-track for the next few miles, which didn't leave me much room to make a move and get back in the race. I wasn't there to win this race, nor did I have any chance to place on the podium, but I did see myself battling for a top-10 position if the race went well. This would now be very difficult as my wrong turn dropped me to 150th place.

The start of the Arizona Trail was so tight and narrow that it presented some serious problems for me being at the very back of the pack. While I was conserving energy in the early miles, I was also losing a ton of ground on the leaders. I started to make my way down the single-track trail only to find there was nowhere to go.

At this point, I found it necessary to pass people any way I could, and that often meant trying to go around them in the boulders or through the deep brush. This wasn't the best idea and my legs were paying the price for it every time I crossed through one of the bushes or rolled my ankle on a rock.

Five miles into the race I saw a slight opening as we moved

downhill. I decided to push the pace of the other runners and check their motivation. Did they want to come along or were they happy to let me go? They were concentrating so hard on the rough terrain that the last thing on their minds was increasing their pace, so I was able to get past them.

I was able to pass a few more runners who were also being very careful on the rocky terrain, moving up to around 100th place. I made my way through the mountain and knew an aid station awaited me at mile seven. This was going to be the first aid station that was open to crews and my wife would be there waiting for me with food to help keep me fueled. I had told her before the race started that I expected the first seven miles would take me 65 to 70 minutes depending on the terrain, so when she saw a hundred runners come through and not one of them was me, she got a little worried. My friends ran past the aid station earlier and checked in with her, briefly telling her that I must have beaten her to the aid station because I was way out ahead of them. Luckily she waited to make sure, and at the 85-minute mark I finally reached the seven-mile aid station.

I could see the look of anguish on her face as she saw me and I shook my head in disappointment at my position in the race. I had no time to stop at this aid station and talk strategy, but I told her what had happened and that I wasn't going to let it bother me. After refilling my stomach with a turkey and cheese rollup and hearing encouraging words from Traci, I was off to continue down a gravel road.

The brief 30 seconds that my wife got to see me at the aid station shows the devotion it takes to be a crew member and follow an ultra-runner. She traveled south with me and began a long day of guessing and waiting for me at various aid stations, only to see me for a few seconds before packing up and quickly rushing to the next station. Constantly waiting for me to arrive and guessing on my whereabouts became the pattern she would follow throughout the day. Until mile 25 (28 miles on my watch with the extra three miles) she would sit and talk to other runners' crews, but would spend the majority of the day guessing where I was and how I was faring. There were aid stations about every five to seven miles but none of them would be accessible by crew until later in the race, because of the terrain and access.

As I made my way down the forest road after mile seven I felt revived and ready to make up some ground on the rest of the field. I knew from looking at the elevation map that miles 7–14 were pretty uphill, but shortly after I would have a four-mile stretch of downhill where I could really make up time. I banked on using my downhill speed to pass other runners. I pushed myself harder than I would have liked to on the uphills but passed many runners. My heart rate was elevated and I felt winded but I was still moving well.

I finally caught up to several people I knew around mile 10. They were baffled as to how I was behind them when I had taken off with the first two groups. We had a brief conversation and I got more words of encouragement along with a little razzing for getting lost. I took the jokes lightly since I often made fun of my own self for getting lost. The truth is I can barely find my way around city streets, let alone difficult trails that darted through the mountains.

I was able to pass a few runners on the hills between miles 10 and 12 and then walked the really steep parts to the top of the summit. I saw the rest of the field walking and knew I could make up a little ground if I just hiked a little faster. I leaned forward, putting my hands on my quads, and began to power-hike up to the top. Since I was pushing the pace, and several runners were struggling with the long climb, I continued to make progress on the rest of the field.

I took one long drink out of my hydration pack and decided it was time to go into an all-out sprint until I reached the bottom of the mountain. I was excited to learn that it actually lasted about five miles and with the field of runners making their way downhill in front of me it was like a game of Pac-Man. I mentally made a plan to pick off one runner at a time.

When you're running an ultra, it is all about the short-term goals, such as making it to an aid station in a certain time. This time I wanted to count 30 runners as I made my way down the gentle gliding forest road. There was another aid station at mile 18. There, I grabbed a Mountain Dew, a handful of pretzels, and some potatoes with salt before jumping back on the trail.

This was before I realized that taking in excess amounts of sodium actually had no impact on one's ability to ward off cramping, but does have a direct correlation to how much water you need to drink. The more sodium you put in your body, the more water is required to maintain a healthy balance. Almost immediately after leaving the aid station we encountered what seemed to be 30-mile-an-hour wind blowing directly into our faces and for the next five miles I thought I was right in the middle of a haboob.

With the arid climate of the southwest we receive heavy winds that pick up the dust from the ground, creating a brown cloud over the sky. These storms (called haboobs) move slowly across the deserts, leaving you feeling battered and gasping for air as the dust flies through the sky. I battled through this section, passing several people who were walking. I mentally took myself to the mile 25 aid station where I knew Traci would be waiting with Gatorade, food, and some instant sugar-candy. After we passed mile 24.5 we had a short downhill section before I could see her. I could see all the cars parked in the distance, reactively turning my pace into a sprint. I wanted to shave a little more time and see if I could disrupt a few runners' races by cruising into the aid station with a large smile on my face. I know from experience that it is often a runner's worst nightmare to see someone running well when they're hurting.

When I arrived Traci let me know just how much time I had made up, leaving me around 12th place overall. I had gone from dead last in the race when the single track started at mile two to just outside the top 10. I was stoked! Her telling me that motivated me. I instantly felt great and had now completed the distance of a full marathon. I only had to continue on for the distance of a second marathon and I would be done.

She let me know that the next four miles were straight uphill and reminded me to take it easy, suggesting I eat some food while I was walking. Cars travelling downhill to the aid station kicked back the road dust for the runners to breathe in. This was a simple reminder that most of the highs one feels in this type of a race are often followed shortly by some sort of low, even if it's as simple as a cloud of choking dust.

I ran the stretches that I could, shuffled through a few other sections, and walked fast in the really steep parts. I checked in with Traci again at mile 29 and fueled up because there would be no more crew access till mile 40. I still felt okay and, to my delight, food still tasted decent. I quickly grabbed more potatoes, a tiny bit of turkey sandwich, some hard candy and gummy worms and I was on my way. I tried consuming 500 calories an hour to keep my body fueled, with only 200 calories coming from liquids. I needed to get some kind of food down.

After I ate, I started to feel the rumble in my stomach and knew the only hope I had of fixing my stomach issue was to take some Tums. I popped about five, and after a few minutes I seemed be feeling good enough again to get my legs moving again.

There would be one last aid station before mile 40. To my delight, it came up quickly at mile 33. This was just a quick stop for me where I slammed a warm cup of Mountain Dew. As I left the aid station, I threw some cold water on my face to cool me down for the final stretch. This was a large section of climbing as we went from 4,600 feet of elevation to 5,800 feet of elevation. I looked at my watch every few minutes, reveling in the fact that I completed more and more elevation gain with every glance.

Upon summiting the climb I relaxed into a brief downhill section before heading into an area of rolling hills. Beeping at every mile, my watch sounded its familiar tone as it read mile 40. Little did my watch know I was still three miles from the mile 40 aid station because of my earlier detour. A familiar mixture of doubt, panic and anxiety began to brew as I thought back to the missed turn onto the Arizona Trail hours prior.

Keeping true to my words to Traci at mile 25, I pushed the negative thoughts away, and it must have worked because just as I did I saw a sign to get me back on track.

"One mile until the mile 40 aid station."

I continued to shuffle down the road until I saw another sign.

"1/2 mile until mile 40 aid station."

As I drew closer, I was sucked in by flags cutting the wind, music pulling my lifeless legs forward and the sight of the best sign of the day.

"Only 10 miles till buckle time."

I thought back to the mental space I'd cleared for the buckle. I set aside any negative thoughts, extra miles and stomach cramps, and made room for new personal bests in distance. Just months before, I was the fat guy getting strange looks from the fit yoga ladies at boot camp and now I had just crossed a sign saying I had run 40 miles, and was on my way to finishing 50.

My excitement level rose again when I saw Traci at the end of the trail, taking pictures as I drew closer. I started to yell, "I'm going to make it, only 10 miles to go!" Refueling my body with some sugar in the form of Jolly Ranchers, I was off to set a new personal mileage goal. On top of this, I was just a mere 10 miles from earning my first coveted belt buckle.

It is amazing how the body pumps adrenaline through your veins so quickly and is able to force it out at a seemingly faster rate. I experienced this immediately upon leaving the mile 40 aid station as I faced a purely uphill battle.

I ran down the forest road for about two miles before hitting the single-track trail that would lead us back up through the mountain range. I glanced at my watch to check the elevation and I was sitting at 5,800 feet. I knew that was the tallest peak at this point of the race and a nice steady downhill section had to be coming soon. I went out too hard in this downhill section and realized I was actually getting slower the harder my body worked. My legs were tired and felt heavy, so using more energy was anything but helpful at this point.

My mind was racing a little as we encountered our first of eight water crossings and I began to sink into a little funk. Several runners began to pass me as I now resorted to walking the single-track portion around the mountain, trying to convince myself mentally that I could suck up the pain and get moving. I kept telling myself how great it would feel to just finish this race and hold that shiny brass buckle in my hands. Knowing that eventually I would set a new personal record for distance, I found myself constantly looking at my watch and as it registered 46.3 miles, I had now gone farther than I had ever gone before. My previous record for 46.2 miles was 9:24:53. This time

I crossed this invisible barrier in 8:38.

My confidence went through the roof at this point and I figured even if I had to walk it in from here I would make it in 10.5 hours. Even though 10.5 hours was not my original goal, I made some mental readjustments due to the extra mileage. With nothing but time on my hands, I mentally graphed the highs and lows of the race. Coming off the high of setting a new personal mileage record, I sank to a new low as a couple of runners I recognized passed me while I walked. These were runners that I previously had a very large lead on and now they were passing me. My dinking around cost me lots of extra time. I now had a new goal that was to cross the 49-mile mark on my watch and get to the mile 46 aid station before the 9-hour, 15-minute mark.

I was successful as I rolled into the aid station. Just as I thought I had overcome my lowest point by reaching my new goal, the demons began to creep in. I threw off my hydration pack, lay down on the ground looking to avoid a pity party, but I was deep in a mental funk. The volunteers offered me food and I accepted but everything tasted so bland and dry and my stomach didn't seem to like anything.

Despite my pity party, the volunteers kept telling me that I was moving well, looking great and that there were only six miles to the finish. That was when I cracked: How could there be six miles left to go in a 50-mile race from the mile 46 aid station? The race I signed up for was 50 miles, not 52! My mind kept telling me how great it would be to see someone I knew, hop in their car and drive off with my head down into the sunset.

Your mind tells you all kinds of crazy things during these events but luckily you can usually talk yourself through the dark moments. I grabbed a couple oranges, ripped the headphones out of my ears and tossed them in my pack before battling the final section of the race. The headphones were really bothering me at the time and the music wasn't soothing at all because I couldn't keep pace with the rhythm of the song.

After crossing a couple more small washes and climbing through a gate, I came upon some spectators who gave me the encouragement to go on. They said that the trail was pretty flat from there in and I would only have about four miles to go. I took a gel, and started to run step by step until my mind won and would tell me to walk. We ran through a small wooded section leading to a parking lot and the end of a seemingly unending trail. This was such a false sense of security because my watch said 53 miles and I could see the end. I yelled as loud as I could because I actually thought it was going to be right around the corner and maybe my Garmin watch was just wrong.

The truth was, the trail started to wind away from the cars, only leaving the sight of another single-track trail through the tall grasses, with no end in sight. I took a look at my watch as it beeped mile 54 and my time was 9:38. I still had a chance to break 10 hours if I hurried and stopped dogging it to the invisible finish line. My legs started to feel light since I knew the end had to be near and I ran as fast as my body would let me go at the moment. I felt like I was flying but it was more like a 10-minute-a-mile pace, if I was lucky.

As I turned the corner, I finally saw the gate I had longed for the entire day. I was greeted by a boy who opened the gate for me and a small crowd yelling that I was about to break 10 hours. As I rounded the final corner, breathing extremely hard, I saw one last person sitting on a rock. "How much farther?" I said. He laughed and said "You have 100 meters; I think you can make it."

I yelled out, "I did it!" as I finished the Old Pueblo 50 (or what I would call the Old Pueblo 55.5) in 9 hours 56 minutes and 32 seconds.

The finish line greeted me with my first racing buckle, a coffee mug reading "second-place male in the 30-39 age group" and 21st place overall.

Demons aside, I couldn't have imagined how good it felt just to finish, let alone to come back from so far behind. I had just run my farthest distance and accomplished more than I ever thought possible for myself. The feeling of finishing a great race stayed with me for a couple days. Then I started to think of my next race and ways to get even faster.

Chapter 15: Oval Torture Chamber

After two years of running track, I still hit the "oval torture chamber" every Tuesday, and while I'm not always excited to run out of my comfort zone it has taught me a thing or two about patience.

You don't start off fast overnight; it takes time to program your body to adjust to new activities. Just as I didn't run 50 miles in my first day on the trails, I didn't run a six-minute mile consistently my first day at the track.

You don't get better by practicing the exact same way every single day. Following my coach's instructions allowed me to make progress and focus on different aspects of running. He took my fear out of running fast and running fast for long distances. Also, having the great support of others around me gave me the encouragement to go out and run harder.

With John's assistance, I continued to attend the Tuesday morning/evening track groups. Ranging from sprinters to marathon runners, each runner had one purpose: speed.

Unexcited by speed, even less thrilled about track work, I began to wonder why I was there. Yet I stuck it out and really began to see a difference in my turnover and pickup. I would find myself arriving at the track and lying down on the ground, looking for pity that an ultra-runner was out doing mile repeats. I didn't want to take my time and build up my speed; I wanted to be fast right away. The problem was that when the workout became too difficult, I was ready to throw in the towel. It took me some time to learn a different side of the sport and when I did, it really began to open up my eyes about my potential.

Most people who set out to run 50 or 100 miles are just looking to finish. John knew my goal and explained that pushing me with weekly speed work on a track would increase my leg turnover. This would in turn make me more efficient and make running in the upwards of 100 miles seem easier.

It helped that my coach would pair me up with runners who were usually just a touch faster than me or around the same level. This motivated me to stay with them as we circled the oval track time and time again. Two or three other days during the week, I would meet up with groups who would run long distances on the roads. I cringed at the thought of running on a road. In my mind, everything about hitting asphalt or pavement was a disappointment. There would be cars to dodge, traffic lights to stop and start back up at, and no beautiful desert vegetation, and something about seeing the road stretched out in front of you seemed to make the run seem longer.

When I was on a trail, I could take in the views as I summited the mountains; weaving back and forth on the path kept my mind busy enough to not worry about how long I would be running. Under John's coaching, my mileage slowly started to increase.

I would open the schedule he sent to my email at the start of each month and mentally prepare for the hardest workouts. I had previously run at least four miles each day, totaling a whopping 28 for the week, occasionally adding extra when I felt like it. But now, with a new focus and a coach to keep me honest, it was not uncommon to have 100-plus mile weeks! This, coupled with new pains I was feeling from speed work and running on the streets, caused me to have feelings of self-doubt. I wondered if I could keep up this type of routine or whether it would get to my mind and body before I even had a chance to enter a 100-mile race.

When I would speak to John about my concerns, he would always point out the positives in my training and would let me know if there was anything he thought I could work on to make things easier. If I was really exhausted after a particularly long run or intense track workout, he would give me the option of taking a day off or lowering my mileage. While I appreciated the idea of a day off, I was in the middle of a running streak that I couldn't forget about, so I pressed on.

It had now been 535 days in a row and I continued to run at least the bare minimum four miles each day—even when I was mentally and physically drained.

Eventually I could tell that my legs were getting stronger, but the pains in my calves seemed to be mounting by the day. I started to wear medical-grade compression socks to bed, instead of just to run. I tried massages and foam rolling, but the knots in my calves were so deep that I began to worry whether the pain would require me to take a few days off, ending my streak. No. I wasn't going to let that happen. I decided to shut out the pain and concentrate on staying true to my goal. I adjusted my mindset by only looking at the next day's workout on my schedule and not the entire week which often felt daunting. Seeing 90-plus miles in a week with tired legs exhausted my mind much more than seeing eight or 10 for the next day.

As we moved into June and 115 degrees started to become the normal temperature in Phoenix, I began to look at the temperature as a challenge. If I was able to run 30 miles in 115 degrees, there was no doubt in my mind I could go to South Dakota in late August and run a strong race.

With a 6 am temperature of 90 degrees, most runners do not look forward to summer training in Phoenix. If I was training for the Badwater race (135-mile race in Death Valley, Calif. in July) then this would have been the optimal training weather, but I was training to run in South Dakota. The temperatures in South Dakota for that time of the year looked to average around 85 degrees for a high, giving me a sense of comfort even during the hottest part of the day.

As the miles on the schedule increased, I became more worried about spending time away from home. To combat this problem, I began training at 3 am. I could barely extend my bedtime to 7:30 pm because I was trying to be at the trailhead early in order to get 30-plus miles in for my long runs. Even though Petra was only three at the time, I was still going to bed before her.

When training for a marathon the average runner will spend 16 to 20 weeks in preparation. In order to fully prepare for a hundred miles, you're looking at eight to 10 months to dial in the distance.

My schedule looked pretty similar each week of the summer. My typical schedule was: Monday: eight miles; Tuesday: 10 to 12 miles with six miles of track workout; Wednesday: six miles; Thursday was a 12-mile hilly tempo run; Friday: 16 to 20 miles; Saturday: 30 to 40 miles; and Sunday would be my semi-recovery day with just four miles.

While lots of runners complete more miles than this each week, it was the back-to-back long runs that really seemed to take a toll on my body. Yet I came to understand that this was one of the greatest ways to train for a race of this magnitude because your body needs to know what it feels like to run when you're not only tired but exhausted. There are other ways to simulate the mental and physical pain the body will go through in 100 miles, but this was by far the best method for me.

Since I would be running through the night in South Dakota, it was important to get my body used to running at all hours. At this point, I had completed a couple races where I ran all night, but really struggled to dial in my nutrition and to stay awake. Knowing this was a deficit, I purposely scheduled one long run every couple weeks beginning at 10 pm. Even though I had run earlier in the day, I counted this run as the next day's miles, as I did not stop until finishing 30 miles the next morning.

Running in the dark tends to be slower and more mentally and physically challenging. Yet I had a theory that putting in these long strenuous miles would pay off as other runners in South Dakota became tired.

For months I continued running 80–100 miles each week. My calves began to ache due to the daily pounding from increased mileage. The knots in my legs got worse and worse and I got worried. I could feel the knots developing in my legs and I knew it was time to back off the mileage. John knew taking a day off was not an option, so he backed my mileage down to 50–60 miles for one week out of every three in a training cycle.

This change helped me to release the mounting leg pressure. After each down week, I felt stronger and faster. I did worry that the decrease of mileage each third week might impact my time at the 100-mile race, but overall, finishing South Dakota one, maybe two, hours slower than I initially hoped for was irrelevant to me. Finishing 923 straight days for T was the most important so I needed to keep my legs in working order.

By August I was at the peak of my training. With just a few weeks until race day, John advised me to back off the long runs, never logging more than 20 miles in one day. John knew I wasn't going to rest, so he simply decreased the miles and told me I was beginning an early taper, leading me to race day. According to his expertise, I was to feel better than I had all summer by race day.

I trusted John's advice and collected the miles leading up to my departure for South Dakota. I left Arizona determined to bring back my first 100-mile finisher buckle and to remember my father through running.

Low moments will happen to every athlete but it is how you overcome the low moments that really count. I would suffer and there were several nights during this training cycle that I wanted to quit and walk away but my dad never would have quit and all I could picture was that incredible smile he would have when I was handed my first hundred-mile buckle.

Chapter 16: Seeking a 100-Mile Adventure

Entering a 100-mile race is difficult for a number of reasons. First, you need to qualify for most of these races. Since these races aren't as prevalent as a city 5K, you might have to participate in one that is held in a different state. This means driving or flying and extra days to plan for travel. Further, you should pick a race that fits your strengths. If you are great at climbing, find a race that has a lot of mountain trails. If you usually run in snow, pick a race that will have similar weather conditions. Another thing to think about is which individuals you can recruit to work as your crew. The crew drives ahead to aid stations and prepares food and water bottles to hand you as you come through. They can also be pacers who help push you in the final miles of a race. It might be difficult to find a friend who is willing to travel and spend their entire weekend sitting and waiting at aid stations only to see you actually run for a few minutes here and there. Luckily I have always had family and good friends who have been willing to travel with me as part of my crew.

In looking for a course, I searched for a slightly easier hundred, which would take place at less than 10,000 feet of elevation, since I would have very few opportunities to train at higher elevations. Even though I usually like to subject myself to that kind of climbing, I wasn't quite sure if my body was ready to take on one of the races with 15–30,000 feet of elevation gain combined with running 100 miles. Every time I would look at one of those races I started to question my sanity and wondered if I really enjoyed doing this or whether I was looking for something to prove.

I looked at races in California, Utah, and Colorado. However, appealing to me the most was a smaller hundred-mile race in Hot Springs, South Dakota called the Lean Horse 100. The course consisted of a converted railway transformed into a beautiful trail running through the Black Hills of South Dakota. There was less than 8,000 total feet of vertical gain over the hundred miles and the entire race would take place between 3,500 and 5,000 feet of elevation, fitting well within my plan.

Making sure the actual trail matched the website description, I headed to YouTube to check out videos posted by previous runners and crew members. The videos showed runners very vulnerable while traveling down the exposed trail in the hot sun. It was clear that shade was a major concern, but for someone from the Arizona desert, this didn't rank really high on my list of concerns. There was no way the August heat of South Dakota could compare to my recent 100-plus degree training conditions in Arizona.

In the end, I chose Lean Horse as a starting 100-mile run for several reasons. First, I felt at ease with the terrain and elevation. Next, I knew I would be able to secure a crew or friends and family to help Traci aid me. Finally, I knew I had nothing to prove to anyone. I had begun my journey nearly 18 months before, lifting five-pound weights at a boot camp class, carrying the heavy burden of grief with me. Thinking of these two scenarios made me smile as I realized running was not about proving anything to anyone, but about finding an outlet for my grief, impatience and everyday stress.

Chapter 17: Lean Horse—100-Mile Race

I had been training for a year and a half for a 100-mile race and my goal started with the thinking that when I was ready to run 100 miles I wanted to finish in less than 24 hours.

We arrived in South Dakota on a Thursday morning in August of 2011. While preparing for the race, I read about the Black Hills, which I pictured to be expansive mountain formations similar to my everyday backdrop in Arizona. What I found were rolling hills that did not take over the skyline like back home.

We drove from Rapid City to a small town of 4,500 people called Hot Springs, where I would meet up with my friend Deb Hamberlin, who would also be running the hundred. This was her second hundred-mile race and since she was one of the most influential people in my quest to run ultras, I wanted to make sure we picked out a race we would both enjoy.

We made our headquarters in a large two-story ranch amidst a 500-acre parcel of open land. The views were fantastic; the only thing around as far as the eye could see were horses, cows, burros and a sprinkling of homes. We checked into our house, laid out our running supplies and spoke of the upcoming weekend with great expectations. I had some serious race goals while Deb told me she was just looking to have fun, run a Western States 100 qualifier and finish the race.

Western States is the world's oldest and one of the most prestigious 100-mile races. It has long been known to showcase talent from all across the world in the run from Squaw Valley, California to Auburn, 100.2 miles away. To many ultra-runners, Western States 100 represents one of the biggest endurance challenges in the world. To get into this race a runner must complete selective 50-mile races in less than 11 hours or finish a 100-mile run. This allows runners to be part of a lottery where just 10 percent will get chosen to run.

Deb reminded me how many ups and downs a person can experience in one of these long races. The most important matter I needed to preserve was my mind. When faced with challenges over the next day, I would not give up. I knew it was going to be a long day and night but I continued to tell myself to shake the nerves. This is what I loved and what I had been training for. There was zero doubt in my mind I was ready to join the hundred-mile club.

While my initial thoughts were to finish the race in 24 hours, I was pretty sure as long as I stayed focused I would be able to cross the line around 20 hours. My estimate was from previous 50-mile race times and differences in course terrain. I will admit I did have some fear of running on a relatively flat course for 100 miles. I knew I would feel guilty if I was compelled to walk. When you're running a mountain race, it is rare to see more than the elites running up the hills. Most will hike the hills and try to run the rest of the race. Because your body begs you to shut down later in the race, it becomes important to conserve energy whenever you can along the way. If you ask most ultra-runners they will tell you that they would prefer to have 15,000-plus feet of elevation gain versus a completely flat course. It would be like running four marathons in a row without a break. There are several runners who can do that, but I didn't find myself to be in that class.

Endurance races are extremely hard mentally and it is always important to stay positive and keep your focus. I knew going into this race that if I lost focus early, my race would be over as quickly as it started. I had no dreams of going out and winning this race or even competing in the top five, I was just trying to finish what I had thought was impossible just two years before.

The race started Saturday morning at 6 am from Hot Springs and would take us to Hill City and then back. Eighty-five percent of the race took place on the George Mickelson Trail, Rails to Trails project. Forest service had done an amazing job of transforming the trails into a bustling gateway to Mount Rushmore. The trail runs the entire distance from Hot Springs to Hill City and it is one of the cleanest and softest surfaces I have ever run on. It was hard to find a rock on the path, and as a runner who hates asphalt and concrete, I couldn't have been more pleased with the cushiony, almost track-like feel of the trail.

Runners arrived in droves at the start line. Within minutes the peaceful trailhead was turned into the most happening spot in South

Dakota. Jerry Dunn, a local ultra-running legend, talked for just a few minutes before the race. With 10 minutes until go time, the crowd was as silent as a return flight from Vegas. I took my place in the middle of the crowd of runners, knowing I had the next 20 or so hours to make a move, if the time came.

An ultra-race of this magnitude doesn't typically begin until mile 80, leaving those who pushed the pace early on in trouble late in the race. By now, so many people had offered their wisdom on the hundred-mile race. Most often, I was told I would not be able to bank miles if I started out fast. Getting an early lead wasn't going to assure me a better performance at the end. I didn't necessarily buy into this theory. My mindset was: If you're running 100 miles, you're going to be tired, no matter what pace you start at. Including stops for the day, I planned to run around 12-minute miles.

I looked to Traci and my brother-in-law, Kevin Conte, at the start for some last-minute words of encouragement. Truth be told, I was feeling pretty confident about the day. Naturally, I had some nervous energy, but the moment the race director announced, "Go!" and my blue Inov-8 shoes hit the trail, I felt on top of the world.

As we took off and saw the 50K and 50-mile runners take off for the lead, I reminded myself that no one would control my pace; I controlled myself. Traci and I had worked out a time schedule for me to arrive at each aid station stop throughout the day. If I was lucky I would stay right in that time range. There were two aid stations before crews were allowed on the course and since it was such a comfortable morning, I didn't even think twice about stopping to refill my bottle. I would meet Traci and Kevin for the first time at the 16.9-mile mark, and told them to expect me around 9:15 local time. This would be 3 hours, 15 minutes into the race. In my mind, this was a slow projection, but I also wanted to be conservative to start so I would not experience a complete meltdown later down the path that might take me out of the race.

I just couldn't let go of the fact that I felt so good at the start so my pace kept getting faster and faster and I told myself it would be okay.

Cruising right through the mile 11 aid station, I foresaw a long gradual downhill ahead. While I was unable to estimate the distance, I decided I would run just a little faster until I got into the 16.9 mile aid station where my crew would be waiting. My original plan was to stop at 16.9 and eat for the first time in the day. However, in looking at my watch, I noticed it was only 8:10 am, a full hour ahead of schedule.

In the meantime, my thoughts were broken apart by the loud ringing of a cowbell as one of the 125 residents of Pringle, South Dakota greeted me with a "Welcome to Pringle!" Turning my focus back to my watch and the issue of my early arrival, I worried my crew would not be at the aid station yet. While I reminded myself to let it be, I spotted Traci, early as usual. She and Kevin helped me get the calories I needed by offering me a turkey sandwich and refilling my bag with electrolyte drinks.

In the midst of me taking down a turkey sandwich, we also scrapped our initial plan of meeting at the next aid station. We agreed I was in a good rhythm and decided not to meet until crew access was allowed at mile 28. This way I would be through one of my four marathons and I would have plenty of time to digest the food.

After finishing the sandwich, I took off from the aid station and into the hot South Dakota sun. Since this was a Rails to Trails project and it ran alongside the highway, it was very easy for crews to keep an eye on their runners the entire day. Occasionally you would duck behind some rock formations, but the majority of the time they spotted me as they drove past at 60 miles an hour. While it was starting to warm up outside, it still was nothing compared to what I was used to in Arizona.

As I ran down the Mickelson Trail, my energy level was up, there was no pain anywhere in my body and I had finished the first of my four marathons of the day in 3:42. Since I would be running the distance of four marathons, I was pretty excited about where I stood in the race.

When I was just a couple miles from the 28.4 mile aid station, I decided it was time to get in some extra calories. I had eaten 12 miles prior but had learned from my previous 50-mile races that if I didn't eat early, and often, I wouldn't have any fuel later on in the race. The thought of taking down another sandwich made me feel sick so my plan was to drink an excessive amount. This was possibly my only mistake of the day because I tried to cram 900 calories into one aid station stop. I drank a recovery drink, my go-to during a race, which consisted of 320 calories, a synthetic food known as a liquid shot which was 400 calories, and then tried to take down a large energy drink which was an additional 210 calories.

At the time I felt okay, but within seconds the jostling in my stomach was so intense, I could barely bring myself to walk out of the aid station. Had I already blown my race based on one poor decision? The recovery drink and liquid shots didn't seem to be the problem, but the addition of the sweet energy drink put my stomach over the edge. I hunched over as I left the aid station, barely moving at a snail's pace down the trail.

The next section was basically an out and back on asphalt bike path to get the total mileage for the day to work out to 100. I wasn't a huge fan of this part of the course as we left the Mickelson Trail to head out to asphalt sidewalks to levy the final mileage to 100. Despite the fact that this section's distance was short the rolling hills and current status of my stomach did not agree. After ascending the first hill, I could feel the sloshing in my stomach so I leaned over a bridge hoping to purge the extra liquid. After a few fruitless attempts, I continued to make my way over the short bridge and tried to change my attitude.

I hoped a shift in attitude would also shift the excess fluid in my stomach to just the right spot to allow me to continue on. I slowly shuffled through this section. On my way back down the asphalt, I passed the first female as I reversed my direction on the out and back course and headed toward the finish. Deb had not made the 50-mile turn yet and as I passed her going the other direction I let her know she was only two miles back of the leader. Deb and I exchanged words of encouragement. Deb looked unbelievable at this point, as if she had just started running five minutes before. I, on the other hand, still struggled with an overabundance of fluids.

After seeing Deb come through, my mindset quickly changed back to positive thoughts. I was extremely happy for her to be so close to one of the premier female runners on the course. Previous to the race, Deb had suffered through some nagging injuries, causing her to not perform at the level I was used to seeing. The good news was, there was no sign of injury as she passed with a huge smile on her face. Seeing Deb moving so well reenergized me.

As my shuffle transformed into a jog and finally a solid running pace, I again realized how something so minute, such as seeing a familiar face, could be more powerful than any energy drink.

Riding out the high of Deb's status in the race, my focus remained strong. I rolled through a few more aid stations before picking up my pacer, Kevin, at mile 47.9.

While you normally must wait until mile 50 to pick up a pacer, course logistics allowed runners to have pacers a little sooner. After a brief meeting between Traci, Kevin and me on how I was feeling and what I would need, we hit the trails. I told Kevin to feed me a Tums every 15 minutes; even if I said no, I told him to force it down. I don't know if it was the Tums or the addition of company, but by the 50-mile mark I had not only set a new personal record of 8 hours, 22 minutes, but I was also no longer suffering from any stomach issues.

Lean Horse was Kevin's introduction to the world of pacing and ultra-running. I enticed him to join my crew through the same videos I watched prior to the run. Even though he had no idea what to expect coming into the event, you would have thought he had been doing it forever after the first mile.

We exchanged stories, talked football and a few laughs. When the laughter turned to whining about the pain in my ankles, he quickly set some ground rules for me. I was only allowed to whine or be negative if I was running. As soon as I began walking, all negativity had to cease. His new rule allowed my mind to focus on running so I could have someone to complain to. Testing his ability to stay committed to his own rules, I tried complaining during a few of our walks. True to his word, he immediately shut me up by running ahead. I grumbled in my own mind, but pressed on.

At 52.9, Tere was briefed on my status and immediately began rattling off my place in the race, the places of other runners and her goal for the next 11 miles of pacing. After a day of crewing, Tere's competitive nature kicked into overdrive and the pace she was trying to hold me to was a little quick. I'm pretty certain my telling her to slow things down only took her to the next gear, because shortly after, I looked down at my Garmin and we were running a 10-minute-mile pace.

Navigating through rocks and crossing more bridges, I became enamored by my surroundings. Not wanting Tere to miss the beauty of the background, I told her to take a quick look at the face of Washington on Mt. Rushmore. The beauty of the mountain didn't seem to impress Tere and I wondered why she wasn't in awe of this national landmark. I wished I had a camera to capture the beauty of what I was seeing. It wasn't until after the race that I understood why Tere was so nonchalant about Mt. Rushmore. Tere's seemingly careless response was because what I had thought was a cutout of Washington in the mountain was actually the Crazy Horse monument. We were well over 30 miles from Rushmore! Shows you how tired I must have been. I couldn't tell the difference between the face of our first president and Crazy Horse. In fact, I was later told we had passed a large sign saying Crazy Horse Memorial. Chalk it up to being a good friend or a sympathetic pacer, Tere let me believe what I wanted to at the time because it seemed to motivate me.

I picked up Kevin at the next aid station to pace me through the next few miles.

Miles 60–72 seemed to fly by as Kevin and I made up ground on a few runners in front of me. As an added bonus, I was able to keep solid food down. I complained a little, walked a little, and then noticed Kevin jogging continuously while looking at his watch and encouraging me to run the next section. I reminded him there was no hurry; we would catch the next runner. My words reached him too late, as Tere had already gotten to him at the last aid station. She told him to run alongside of me even when I was walking to encourage me to pick up my feet and keep moving. They planned not to let me run less than 11.5-minute miles during this section, so I could pick up some ground on the next group of runners.

Kevin and I ran pretty well during this stretch. While I wasn't any farther away from the runners in front of me, I wasn't much closer either.

Tere was raring to go by the next aid station. It was clear she had a plan and was ready to execute. Right away, she hit the gas and we passed the fourth-place runner. Having been passed in previous races, I knew how mentally crushing it is to hear, "Nice job, looking good!" as a runner passes you. Not wanting number four to think he could pass me back, I gave him the standard, "Nice job, looking good" and smiled to Tere. We made a large move late in the race, but in no way could become comfortable.

After making the move to fourth place, my crew took on a different attitude. While other crews seemed to be laughing and joking, enjoying the spread of food and drink, mine informed me what was available ahead of time so I wouldn't waste any time when I got to the aid station. There was no way they would let me waste time talking and mulling over food this late in the race. They had been out there all day, too, and wanted to see me finish strong.

Leading the charge, Traci took my two empty water bottles and immediately handed me two spares. Jealous of those appearing to have a good time, I continued to plod along toward the end of the Mickelson Trail.

Finishing this section, daylight became pitch-black, replacing sunlight with shooting stars. This time not a figment of my imagination, the beauty of the course sank in, leaving me to think of the journey my life had taken. However, I knew better than to daydream too far away from reality as I was quickly approaching the worst section of the run: miles 83–95.

At mile 83, I picked up Kevin for the dreaded Argyle Road section. Ultra magazines warned that while the trail does not switch to an asphalt road, you do have to travel along a gravel road for over 11 miles. While this normally would not have been a big deal, and probably would be a welcome relief from the rocks I normally run, my already banged-up feet told my mind they didn't want to deal with a dirt track.

It's funny how you can dread something all day, but once you are finally in the moment you realize you have no other choice but to move forward. Kevin helped me with the decision to move forward as he grabbed a handful of espresso beans and salted potatoes to aid us down the lonely country road.

Knowing I had a decent lead on the runner Tere and I had passed, I told Kevin I needed to take my time. We knew this section would be all rolling hills with a 1,500-foot descent. Even though I never felt any of the descent, we continued to shuffle the flats, run the downs, and walk the ups. It was all I could do to maintain pace and try to get off this road. We tried entertaining ourselves with jokes and yelling at imaginary wildlife, but the truth was we both had had enough by the time mile 95.1 rolled around. Completing this section in about 2.5 hours, I became glad I had banked time early in the race.

While familiar faces earlier in the race made me smile, I felt my mental state beginning to weaken. This was especially true as crew cars (including my own) drove by and dusted Kevin and me. Words of encouragement shouted from the windows of my own crew car no longer worked to encourage me. All I could think of was getting to mile 95 and back on the trail.

The long-awaited mile 95 was so welcoming. We finally left the road and headed up a rocky trail to the last aid station. I grabbed some chips, took a shot of Mountain Dew and said "Let's finish."

There was one issue. My shins and ankles hurt so badly I could barely put together a shuffle. Now armed with both Kevin and Tere as pacers, my complaints would not be heard. I mean literally: they decided to run 50 yards ahead of me as a ploy to get me to move faster.

While I cursed their existence on the inside, I struggled to formulate cohesive sentences on the outside. However, I knew I was almost done. At this point, it was hard for me to fight back tears as I kept saying, "This is for you, T." While T had no idea what a hundred-mile race was and would never have envisioned me running one, I wanted this so badly for him. Since his passing I had transformed myself into a man he might not even believe if he were here today. Both physically and emotionally unrecognizable from the man I had been, I knew T would be proud of my efforts today.

As we weaved our way through the town of Hot Springs, we asked a motorcyclist, "Which way to the Dairy Queen?" Knowing this was our last landmark next to the finish line, we were all eager to finish the race. I glanced up, with a half mile to go, to where the town clock read 12:56 am; my hopes of finishing in less than 19 were all but out the window. I yelled ahead to Tere and Kevin, "I just need a moment, leave me alone." Tere said, "Come on, you are almost done!" and kept running beside Kevin. I yelled at the top of my lungs that they were the worst pacers ever. This was supposed to be a fun run for them; they were there to help me. They continued to run ahead and try to bring me in for a strong finish. We rounded the corner and saw the Dairy Queen, followed by a stream of glow sticks at the finish.

The glow sticks guided us through the finish where I heard Traci screaming, "Come on Danek!" Tears streamed down my face as Tere and Kevin moved out of the way so I could sprint through the line. I sprinted and leaped up, smacking the clock as it read 19:01:12. Had I not taken my moment I would have been sub-19. The clock in the city was fast, and I threw in the towel early. I can honestly say the extra 01:12 didn't bother me. I mean, I had originally set out to run 20:00 and now I was nearly under 19:00!

I could see the emotion on Traci, Tere, and Kevin's faces as they knew I had just done something special and they were an enormous part of it. I had finished my first 100-mile race in fourth place, with a finisher's time of 19:01:12. I was ecstatic.

So what happened to my friends in the race? As I thought, Deb ran the race of her life. She continued to feel great all day. My crew went back and assisted her at the aid stations after I came through to keep her motivated and chugging along. Kevin decided he hadn't had enough fun for one day and after running 33 miles he ran alongside Deb for more. Kevin met her at mile 95.1 and paced her in for the last five miles. I think his presence lifted her up and she knew she was about to do something special. We all gathered at the finish line at 2:30 am to see Deb cross as the first female finisher of the day! First place in only her second 100-mile race ever! She was truly awesome all day and the second female was now over an hour back. My time and finish quickly became irrelevant because I had just watched my friend win her first 100-mile race. I knew the pain it took to win and I was so proud of her.

Lean Horse taught me several lessons about running and life. To begin with, ultra-running is not an individual sport. More importantly, it is about giving back to others as my crew selflessly did for me for 19-odd hours. In the end, it's not just about your personal victories, but also about those of the runners you train with. While the sub-24-hour buckle is a great way to commemorate a run like Lean Horse, the memories of where I had been and where I had taken myself at this point in my life had more significance to me.

As I pass this buckle on my bookshelf each day, I can only think of the look of amazement T would have had if he were there to witness my finish himself. He supported me in every venture growing up and it is times like these when I miss him most.

Chapter 18: Bonding Time

One of the things I shared with my T was a love of collecting baseball cards. When I wasn't outside practicing baseball with T and my brother Bryan, the three of us would spend hours putting together massive collections of baseball cards. We went to card shows and card shops, and frequented toy stores that sold baseball cards. We would always look for the three-pack cellophane-wrapped cards because T discovered that these packages often had the most sought-after cards containing the superstar athletes. To keep them in mint condition, we rarely opened our baseball cards.

We learned how to identify the order in which the cards were produced. The companies that made trading cards used machines that didn't randomize the card packs. They were actually always in the same order. So, if we had a pack containing a specific player we knew not to buy the same package because we would likely get the same cards we already had. Because of this, we would go to the store with a list of superstars that were high on our list and search through all the packs until we found exactly what we came in for.

Most kids were more interested in the gum that was also included in the card packs, but not us. We were interested in one day opening a large baseball card shop that we could pass down for generations to come. Our hobby lasted from childhood through high school, as we continued to buy and save unopened packs of cards and spend hours together labeling them and getting them ready for sale in the future. This obviously wasn't for everyone but it was my dad's way of trying to teach me patience. He explained that taking the time to do something carefully and slowly up front would lead to great rewards in the future.

I loved to spend money and I still do. It has always burned a hole in my pocket, per se, and I could always find something I needed. Having this asset taught me responsibility, savings, a little patience, all while bonding my brother, T and me.

When we were not collecting cards, T, my brother and I would hit the field for batting practice and endless games of catch. We would go to the park down the street with two five-gallon buckets of baseballs and take batting practice for hours. When we got tired of shagging the balls from the fields, we would ask T to take us to the batting cage and the answer was always yes. He saw the potential in us and knew that hard work and time would not only make us better athletes, but better people.

Baseball was my escape from school, and it was my way of capturing the excitement many kids felt from playing athletics.

My mom and dad showed up at every baseball game I played. I always felt confident when I saw him in the crowd cheering me on. I was not an average baseball player growing up in Michigan; I was considered to be an up-and-coming talent that would follow right in my brother's footsteps. Most people expected me to play college baseball. My brother was a star second baseman his whole life and knew every intricacy of the position. He knew how to manage every situation that would arise during a game. He taught me the game from his perspective, but we were different. I sought the spotlight whereas Bryan was quiet and reserved.

I think a sign of a good baseball player is that one can play a number of different positions. Because I felt that way, I worked hard and learned how to play third base, shortstop and even pitcher. There was something about baseball that always brought out the fearlessness in me. I remember a 14-year-old boy who threw 75-mile-an-hour pitches that intimidated everyone, but not me. My attitude was—bring it on! I was up for the challenge.

I think in a way I was constantly trying to prove myself and shed the label "Danek's little brother." After years of hearing I was "too slow," "too tall," "weak with the curve ball," and "clumsy"—even though I was hitting for average, pitching for strikeouts and fielding every ball that came my way—I developed a bit of a chip on my shoulder. I wondered if I'd ever get a chance to showcase exactly what I'd do for the team if I was always being held back by others' judgments.

My dad saw the fight in me. He knew how hard I worked, and I always loved hearing him tell me he was proud of me after every game.

Unfortunately, one summer day after years of playing ball,

something happened that brought my excitement for the game to an end. I loved the game, loved to practice, and loved to be around my teammates. What I didn't love was the way my 12-year baseball career came to an end. It wasn't an injury but rather an encounter with my coach that changed the way I felt. He thought it was better to use a bad high school decision I had made to embarrass and cut me down in front of my entire team and he did it daily. His intent was to show the kids "what not to do."

I fully admit that what I did was by all means not a good decision and that other kids should not follow my lead, but to be reminded of it daily was more than I cared to handle.

Chapter 19: My Biggest Fan

I was never particularly fond of high school. When you're growing up, older friends refer to high school as the best time in their lives, but I never understood what was so great about it. In high school most people are still trying to find themselves and it is the first time you see real segregation between groups of people. You might have fit into one or two different groups, but it seemed like certain people like the jocks always stayed together. I spent a lot of my time with fellow baseball players but I found that I fit in better with friends who played sports recreationally.

I began to spend less and less time with my teammates when we weren't on the practice field. I was now hanging out with a group of friends that I more closely resembled and I finally felt like I fit in. Since we were all free spirits, we often found ourselves in some precarious situations. But I couldn't blame my friends for any trouble I got into. My anxiety and lack of patience always caused me to make hasty decisions.

When I found myself dreading to go to class, the quick and easy answer was for me to skip out. Playing pickup basketball at the gym seemed like a much better option than sitting through a boring history class. Besides, after years of never missing classes, I learned that each student was allowed 10 absences per semester, so I quickly took advantage. History bored me and learning a new language seemed pointless, but playing 5-on-5 in the gym was all the rage. I knew what my grades needed to be in order to graduate and made sure to keep them at that level, but I never saw the point in taking the extra effort studying subjects that I would quickly forget.

Teachers would call home and inform my parents that I missed class and to them I would always say, "They wouldn't give us 10 absences if they didn't want us to use them." I never wasted the days being sick; instead, I wasted them to play basketball or leave campus with friends. We weren't out getting in trouble; we were just trying to enjoy our freedom away from school.

It was the start of my junior year of high school and several friends and I were looking for a way to escape the monotony of school. I had never been one to drink, but that Friday evening seemed like the perfect time to have a little fun before the high school football game. With the exception of a few sips here or there, alcohol was never worthy of my time. I avoided any situation that would hinder my baseball focus and I feared letting my parents down. Not because I would be reprimanded but because I never wanted to upset or worry my parents. My anxiety always got the best of me, so I worried intensely about the outcome. What if I had a drink and got caught? What if I liked the taste of alcohol? Why couldn't I just be like every other kid and gloss over the consequences and go out and enjoy myself?

Before the game started, several of us met at a construction site where a golf course was being built. We all brought just enough beer and vodka to be too much. I didn't particularly like the taste of beer but everyone told me that after a couple beers I would start to like it, so I decided I'd give it a try. That night I distinctly remember drinking St. Ides Malt Liquor. We had a couple cases full of 40-ounce beers, enough to wreak havoc on seven teenagers. I thought the taste of beer was bad before trying the heavy stuff. (For those of you who are not familiar with malt liquor, it is a beer with higher alcohol content than most.) A good bottle of malt liquor, in my opinion, equates to a skunked cheap beer. My friends were right and after a few drinks I began to tell myself that it was good. I'm pretty sure it wasn't the taste I liked, but how it was making me feel. Anxiety gone. It felt like an incredible escape from the hours of baseball practice and the boredom of school. We were just hanging out talking and having a great time. After three or four beers I began to care less about trying to be "perfect" for my baseball coaches.

That night I drank and drank until my friends didn't quite know what to do with me. I was having difficulty standing and talking. Still, since I was somewhat coherent, my friends assumed I was okay. We hung around the construction site until dark and then decided it was time to head over to the school and meet up with other friends at the game.

Like most high school football games it wasn't about the game itself; it served as a place to meet up with lots of friends and plan the rest of the evening. Seven of us arrived at the stadium just after kickoff. My friends were buzzed, and I was a certifiable wreck. Since this was my first time being "overserved," I had absolutely no idea how to act or, at that point, how to even function. We all sat down in the stands and after a short time I began to get very nauseous and dizzy.

It was at this point that people began to quickly take notice that I wasn't doing well. My friends quickly looked for a way to get me home. We got up from the stands and found a friend who had not been drinking who said she would drive me. My friends assured her that I was okay and although I'd feel miserable tomorrow, she had nothing to worry about getting me home. I stumbled as I made my way down the dirt track next to the bleachers before making one bad fall in front of some police officers. I was incoherent at this point and really had no idea where I was, so when an officer asked me some questions I had no intelligent answers for him. The questions were most likely as simple as: What's your name? What did you drink tonight? Are you okay? Needless to say I couldn't answer any of these questions and I was told that until I could they were going to have to hold me in their police car. How embarrassing. Five minutes seemed like five hours as I sat in the back seat of that car. I kept getting dizzier and more nauseous. The police officers decided they were going to have to drive me out of there because I was just too sick.

Since they were parked towards the end zone of the field, the referees stopped the game when the police officers wailed their sirens to quickly escort me to the closest hospital. There my stomach was pumped for alcohol poisoning. Turned out—not a fun night. The whole school had seen me. To make matters worse, when I woke up in the hospital I had my parents on one side of the bed and my baseball coach on the other. I knew I was going to be in serious trouble.

I was released from the hospital that morning and sent home with my parents, who were as calm as could be. Their calmness was eerie and all I could think was how much I had disappointed them. I could tell by the look in my parents' eyes that this little stunt of mine had really scared them. There wasn't any yelling or questions about what I was thinking; it was silence. Silence was never a good sign, especially when it was coming from my mom and dad. T would try to speak and would stop mid-sentence, clearly frustrated with me and wondering if this was somehow his fault. My mom was still in shock. She had always shied away from alcohol and never found any interest in having more than a sip or two so she didn't understand how this could have gotten so bad.

I was worried about my baseball coach but more worried that I had lost my parents' trust. I quickly learned that they were two people who would never give up on me and were always there to support me through good and bad, but I can't say that for my baseball coach.

When I returned to school, I took the expected razzing from classmates and friends pretty well. After all, it was my dumb mistake so I should face up to the consequences. I also felt a difficult conversation with my coach was looming. We were months from the baseball season but a major infraction like this is never good for someone who plays sports. There was never an alcohol pledge or contract signed by the players promising not to drink, but it was discussed at several team meetings throughout the year and deemed unacceptable.

When I spoke to my coach later that day, I told him that nothing like this would ever happen again and we agreed that I would use this act as a learning experience. He made sure to emphasize how alcohol had messed up so many of his players in the past. I was told that if I was caught drinking again I would be removed from the team. Although I was happy he did not kick me off of the team right then and there, I also became defensive. Why was I the only person being reprimanded for drinking when other members of my team were drinking too?

As baseball season approached, the seniors on the team always took on the task of assigning every player a nickname. An example of this was the name "Browser" for a guy with a thick unibrow. Then there was the name they chose for me that year, "The Malts Fault." I probably could have fought the name chosen for me, but it didn't matter. That nickname was printed on the back of my team shirt.

Every time I saw one of those shirts it made me angrier on the field. I wasn't angry at my teammates for the name but instead angry at my coaches for thinking it was the perfect name. To me it was comparable to being sentenced to wear a sandwich board with your offense on it for six months. Classmates and teachers would ask about the name and I had no choice but to make the best of it

Baseball doesn't start until the spring in Michigan because of the cold winters, but it didn't keep us from practicing inside for groundballs and taking batting practice. Going into the winter of my junior year I could hear the chatter from the coaches that they weren't sure if I would ever recover from this incident and even though I had been suspended from school for a few days they thought I still needed to learn my lesson for tainting the image of the baseball team.

How long were my coaches going to berate me for a stupid night of drinking? I wasn't sure if they were using this to try to motivate me but all it did was piss me off to the point that I began to resent them as coaches. I think that they were also trying to get the point across to the rest of the team that if they chose to make a poor decision, they shouldn't expect to get off easy. Yet I wasn't sure if this was the best way to go about it, since only a few on the team respected them as coaches and most thought they needed to be replaced with someone who had changed philosophies on the game in the last 10 years.

The players talked but most were afraid to voice their opinion. I don't know anyone on the team who would have stood up to let the coaches know that we needed to make changes, but I wasn't scared to share my feelings. When you're already losing interest in the game, you begin to question the motives of others. My teammates expressed their concerns to me and I used them as a defense mechanism when the coaches fired off negative commentary in my direction.

Parents were also critical of me and seemed to look at me like I was the only person who had ever been in trouble before, when in fact I had avoided the temptation from many of my friends for years. The first time I decided I was going to try drinking I went overboard. It doesn't make it right that it was the first time, but I couldn't for the life of me figure out how everyone's parents thought their kids were holier than thou, never having done anything wrong in their lives. I'm not saying they were out partying and getting into trouble, but very few kids in high school are as innocent as they let on. That was nothing new and I'm sure most parents on the team had experienced similar situations when they were teenagers, so I didn't understand why they couldn't look past the incident. The parents began to talk behind my mom and dad's backs about the path I was going down. These were parents of kids I had played sports with my entire life. Several parents wouldn't let my friends be around me anymore because they feared trouble. I lost a lot of respect for some of the parents on the team during that season. Before I was caught drinking they were like family and after I made a mistake they went running for the hills. My parents hadn't changed and this one situation didn't change who I was, but many of the parents saw it as a sign of worse things to come.

During batting practice and running drills, if I ran slower than others, the coaches would make it a point to ask me if I was out drinking the night before, as though I was an alcoholic. There were so many times when I just wanted to tell them where they could go but I used T's motto of patience and tried to just let it roll. The atmosphere wasn't a positive environment and very few team members were happy with the direction the team was going.

The regular season went by without any major hiccups, and while my parents and I were reminded several dozen times about my mistake by the assistant coach, the head coach had finally realized that continuing to talk about it was not going to do anything for my confidence as a player.

When the regular baseball season ended it was time for summer baseball, and this was always one of my favorite times of the year. The atmosphere was a little more relaxed than high school ball. You had the opportunity to play the best of the best while traveling around the state of Michigan. We had faced several of the elite pitchers and players before, but now they were combined on a few teams and we would get a crack at them all at once. That summer I pitched every third game and played third base the rest of the time, but every time I didn't have the game of my life I was hearing about it from the coach afterwards. The coach for summer baseball was the assistant coach during the high school season and it always seemed like he was trying to use me as an example. I could have gone 5-for-5 and he still would have started the post-game speech by telling me that my doubles would have been triples if I would just work on my speed and quit staying out at night. I never quite understood the comment since I wasn't actually going anywhere at night except to sleep, and I lived a pretty boring life.

As the season was coming to a close I had been telling my parents that I might be done playing baseball after the season and it was doubtful that I would return for my senior season of baseball unless there was a change in coaches.

The last thing my dad wanted me to do was quit the team and he knew I had the talent to play college baseball and possibly earn a scholarship if I worked hard. I was willing to give it a try, since I did love the game of baseball, but I was so close to the edge. I told my dad that if I was going to come back I would want to have a sit-down with the coach prior to making that decision. I figured my best chance to talk with him would be after our final game, and since it was just a couple days away I was going to let everything roll off me until then.

We finished up the season with a strong record and I played one of the best games I had played all summer. I felt like I was seeing the ball as clearly as I had all season and nothing excited me more than having the ball hit my way in the field. As the game ended and we celebrated a successful season we gathered for the post-game talk from our coach. As we sat around in a circle, the seniors on the team were announced one by one and thanked for all their time on the team. He next went to the junior class. We had a junior-dominated team and one by one our coach went through and began to tell us a couple things that went well during the season and a couple things we should work on before next spring.

After telling me how strong of a season I had and how my bat really came around during the second half of the year, he approached the final player. As he spoke I began to tune out a little because he wasn't talking to me, but after he went over his goals for next year he said something that lit a fire under me. "Scott, I can see you having a great varsity season as long as you don't go on a drinking binge like

Danek." I absolutely lost my cool. I ripped off my jersey and threw it at my coach. Profanities wouldn't stop coming out of my mouth. I was officially done at this point and nothing he or anyone could say was going to change my mind. While his apologies were rampant and he felt horrible, it was too late. He had lost me as a player and as someone who respected him as a person. As I walked off the field, he tried to chase me down to apologize but there was no use because I didn't want anything to do with him again.

Going home that evening was tough because I was going to have to explain to my parents that I had officially quit playing baseball, the game T and I had shared since I was five. When I told them about what had happened, I expected to hear that maybe I had overreacted, but after a season of abuse that they could hear from the stands, they agreed with my decision to walk away unless there would be another coach. This was not at all how I wanted to end my baseball career but I really didn't see any other way.

That evening we had a knock on our front door and it was my coach looking to come in and apologize. My mom and dad didn't even let him in the house. This was a little out of character for T but he had had enough of hearing about the incident and simply told him my decision was final. I gained a great deal of respect for my father that day. He had stood up for me when I really needed him. He really was my biggest supporter. I had walked away for good at this point and while I wasn't sure in my mind if this was what I really wanted to do, I never swung a bat again or threw another pitch in my life.

Walking away from the game I loved and had spent my whole life playing was extremely difficult but I was content with my decision and there was nothing anybody could say that would change my opinion.

A senior year with no sports leaves a 17-year-old with way too much time, I quickly found out. Looking back, we all need to go through some learning experiences in life that will teach us what we do not want our children to do.

During my senior year, I heard it all from teachers and parents who said things such as "He is hanging around with the wrong crowd" or "It would be in his best interest to go back and play baseball to take some of the free time off his hands."

I don't think it is ever fair in life to blame someone else for things that you did wrong, and saying he is hanging around with the wrong crowd is the perfect example. Who knows, maybe I was the wrong crowd to hang around with or maybe I just had a loss of focus, but the truth is we're all responsible for our own decisions. I could have avoided trouble and if I was doing something that could land me in trouble, my anxiety took over my body. I always looked for ways to suppress my anxiety and doing something out of character never helped. I experimented with different things in high school and peer pressure had nothing to do with it. I have never heard someone say "Come on, just try it." No one cared if you drank or smoked; it was and always will be a personal choice. I think to say it was peer pressure is a cop-out. Nobody made me drink that night at the football game. I decided for the first time in my life that I wanted to feel what it was like to drink and I found out the consequences of overdoing it.

Moderation has never been a strong point of mine. Maybe it started that day when I tilted back three times as many bottles as the rest of my friends, but it took an experience like that for me to gain some insight about myself. I have an addictive personality and it is easy for me to get caught up in the moment. Some say I'm just a passionate individual with an obsessive mind, and maybe those people are right. After running a few ultras and completing my first 100-mile race, I felt addicted and quickly signed up for additional races.

Chapter 20: Dancing in the Dark—Take Two

Only six weeks after completing the Lean Horse 100-Mile race in South Dakota, I signed up for the Javelina Night Run. I wasn't sure if my body was ready for another race so soon, but Traci thought running the Javelina Night Run one year after I had run it as my first-ever ultra would be a great way for me to see how far I had come. So, I figured, why not?

Maybe it was the 99.8 miles of running or possibly the final sprint at the finish line, but one or the other left my body completely wrecked after completing Lean Horse. I could no longer recognize my own feet.

I stuffed the grapefruits I found beneath my swollen ankles into my shoes for days following the race. More important than fully functioning appendages was my faithfulness to the streak. I was now 18 months in, and had no choice but to shuffle out the most painful four miles I was yet to encounter.

Beyond the streak, Traci saw fit to keep me motivated by signing me up for Javelina Jundred in Fountain Hills, Ariz., just 20 minutes from our house. While I had little excitement about completing another hundred-miler so soon after my previous race, it was a chance to run with many of my ultra friends from Arizona.

Since running in my first ultra-event of 46 miles just one year prior, I had now completed a full hundred-mile race. I was a runner who struggled to complete the third loop of the Javelina Night Run just one year prior. That man would certainly not recognize the new me who had just finished my first 100 and would toe the line of the Javelina Jundred.

In theory, the plan was solid. I was already in shape and the race was practically in my backyard, giving me the advantage of knowing the terrain and course. The reality was, my body was tired. I had just completed my first 100-miler, preceded by a year of intense training. While my body longed to tackle 50-mile weeks, I knew putting in so few miles would not yield the results I wanted. Instead, I compromised with my mind. If I trained in the 80-mile range, I promised my legs and ankles to stay off the track and roads. Maybe it was more of a mental game, but this was just the concession I needed to make with my mind.

With my head in the game, I set my sights on setting or at least matching a personal record. After about a week, the swelling in my ankles dissipated. I could finally recognize my feet again. I hadn't lost any endurance over the last week and my legs felt extremely strong.

In preparation for the hundred-mile event, I decided it would be a good idea to sign up for the Javelina Night Run on the same course. The night run was one month prior to the hundred miles. This would serve as a hard training run, but with other runners and volunteers manning aid stations. With all the extra people out there I knew it would motivate me to run fast and get it done.

Standing around the start line, I thought back to the unsure feelings I had had one year prior. Back then I had set my sights on completing three loops, 46.2 miles. Now, a year later, I stood in the same place shooting for four loops, 61.6 miles, in less than 12 hours. While I knew it would be a challenge, I reminded myself of all I had accomplished in that year and it gave me confidence. I was mentally and physically ready to tackle another loop. In listening to the conversations of fellow runners, I knew I would be in good company. Many discussed going for four, only increasing my drive to make the tight cut-off onto the fourth loop. I knew if I had a group of consistent runners who could stay together, we could make this a fun run.

With pure adrenaline flowing like lava, I crossed the first loop which was 25K. I was 30 minutes ahead of schedule. While I reminded myself to plan ahead for four loops, my legs brought me through my second loop about as fast as the first. Before I knew it, I crossed the start/finish line again, ready to grab a pacer and head out for the final two. I had run the first 50K in 4:50, not my fastest 50K time, but well ahead of where I needed to be to finish strong in the 100K. The third loop confined me to third place from start to finish.

As I crossed the aid station and readied myself to head out for a final loop, I saw my opportunity. I saw the exhaustion of the other runners who had gone out way too fast and were not getting back up. Without hesitation, I grabbed my bottle and headed out. Since there was a possibility that either one of them would get up in the next few minutes after resting I didn't want to hold back on my pace. I figured I could use this time to drive ahead and take the lead. Unwavering in my new goal of winning the race, I mentally prepared myself to run my final lap in 2:10.

Unwilling to take my foot off the gas, I pressed forward. Looking back for headlamps, I took the full moon into consideration. Knowing some tactical runners might turn off their headlamps when approaching, I decided it was not time to play games, but to finish strong and fast. (Oftentimes runners will turn off their headlamps and use the full moon for light as they try to sneak up on other runners.) With just three miles to go, I hammered the downhill section, leaving my pacer wondering what he had signed up for. After navigating the semi-rocky terrain, my pacer quickly caught up in the flat section where I asked him to sprint to the finish to warn Traci I would be crossing in no time.

He rounded the corner and ran towards the finish line. I could hear the cheers and cowbells as onlookers yelled the now familiar call of "Runner!" While I was not there to see her face, Traci told me she sank in disappointment knowing a runner was coming. She assumed I had been passed on the final lap. After recognizing it was not a race participant but my pacer, Traci worried something had happened to me out on the course. Was the pacer running ahead to get medical help? Within seconds I emerged from the dark trail and worked my way through the parking lot, which was just before the finish line. The cheers and ovation from volunteers seemed to fuel me as I sprinted through the finish in first place. I had crossed the 100K mark in 10:26. I ended up winning by over an hour! This gave me all the confidence I needed going into the Javelina Jundred, which would be one month later on this same course.

Chapter 21: Javelina Jundred

The Javelina Jundred started on a hot October morning. My familiarity with the course was a good thing and a bad thing. Since I had run it before, I knew I could do it again. However, I often found that the new sights and beauty of other ultras I had run made the time go by faster as I ran. I was a bit worried that this 100-mile race would drag on.

While many of the out-of-town runners camped out, I took my home field advantage to gain extra time pacing my own living room floor. Having never camped in a tent before, I figured the night before my second 100 was not the time to start. When the alarm sounded early, I anxiously crawled out of bed, wondering why I had thought signing up for another 100-mile race was a reasonable idea.

Running long-distance races can put a lot of fear into your mind. Nothing weighed on my mind more than worrying about my 3-1/2-year-old daughter Petra. She loved to come and watch me race and "sell water/food to runners at the aid stations." I have always worried that something could happen to me out on the course and she would be suffering a similar fate to the one that I suffered when my dad passed at 58. Nothing makes me happier or run faster than seeing her smiling face as I come into the aid stations. One time during a 100K event she asked me after my first 50K, "Are you almost done, Dad?" I couldn't help but smile and laugh. It's not exactly easy to explain to a 3-1/2-year-old that you still have 50K to go. Time is pretty irrelevant to a young child. If I know Petra is at the race it eases my mind and allows me to stay focused on the task at hand. When she stays home, I find myself worried that I may never see her smiling face again. I started this race with her by my side, which eased my anxiety as we made our way to the starting line.

I came to the start of this race with a plan of how I would run each mile. The plan was to run 2:20ish for my first 15.4-mile loop of the day and to stay consistent for all seven laps. However, I had to remind myself that in ultras, the sheer distance and pain often derails any plans a participant might make.

Halfway into the first loop I found myself veering off course. I quickly realized my error when I heard a fellow runner and friend call out, "How ironic that the McDowell Mountain Man who runs here every day got lost in his first loop!" (Thanks for the wakeup call and helping me get back on course, Jeremy.) Pain ensued as I followed the path and started to curse my decision to eat a bagel before starting the run. It was not sitting well with my stomach. Despite my rule of never eating before 11 am, let alone before racing, I went ahead and tried to gain some early calories. Sure enough, I quickly found myself stepping off course in order to try to stretch out the stitch in my stomach or possibly use the nearest cactus and boulder for a quick restroom stop. Since I pulled to the side so early in the race, the second group of runners coming up behind me turned around to see if I was okay. I told them to go ahead. Somehow, the brief stop cleared up my pain and I resumed running within a few minutes.

The second loop started with 6.25 miles of gradual uphill. While this climb was tolerable in the beginning of the race, I knew by the end it would be plain torture. Large climbs excite me as a runner, knowing the payoff will soon follow on the descent. However, in this case, the six-mile ascent was met with no downhill compensation. I felt spot-on at this point, yet my earlier stop had pushed me back about three miles behind the leaders.

While I had zero intention of competing in this race when I registered, a few friends and I had created an ultra-running pool and someone had picked me to win. I guess this motivated me, so from time to time during the race I thought about pushing harder and working to get to the front of the pack. Since my current position was not near the front, the poor person who had bet on me thought it was important to tell me how badly I was killing him in the pool by falling so far behind. He was clearly joking and giving me a hard time, but it did bring a smile to my face and got me moving along with a little more ambition.

By the third lap, reality had set in, with pain following close behind. Not only was my stomach turning again, I began to feel mentally anguished for the first time all day. I started to feel nauseous and my body had that weak feeling that so many of us associate with the flu. The first aid station was only 2.1 miles out and I couldn't even make it there before I had to make another stop in the desert. This was deflating both mentally and physically but there is always the hope that once you take care of business you will be okay to move forward. Unfortunately, that wasn't the case on this lap and my next stop came just a half-mile later at the next aid station. This cost me even more time behind the leaders. They offered me food and ginger but I thought the only thing I could do at that point was to try to get some salt in my system. I chomped down on the salt tablets and poured water into my mouth to try and relieve the onslaught of dehydration. In my mind I kept telling myself I would be okay but the truth was I was absolutely miserable and I wanted the day to be over.

Clearly distraught and ill, I made my way back to the course in hopes of finding some company to take my mind off of my physical state. My inability to think clearly, let alone run, was really starting to wear on me. A few elite runners passed as I swayed side to side and they looked like I had hoped and envisioned I would look by that point in the race. I did my best to run alongside them, but when they pressed the pace, my stomach could not follow their stride. Parting ways for the day, I was yet again disappointed with myself for not following through on my original plan.

My hopes of finishing anywhere near my previous 100-mile time quickly faded, leaving me slowly plodding along the trail. Thoughts of accepting a DNF (Did Not Finish) loomed over me.

Having reached this dark space in previous races, I knew the feeling would pass. The challenge was remaining patient, riding out the misery and not letting my physical state impact my mental. Barely moving along and making a couple more brief stops in the desert, I finally made my way to the aid station where the sound of volunteers yelling my name and ringing cowbells helped me regain that feeling of excitement I had had in the days leading up to the start. I slowly ran into the aid station.

Normally aid station volunteers will tell you that you're doing great, nice job, looking good.... I heard no such thing. My shirt was covered with a crusty salt layer, I was sweating profusely, sick, and no one, including the medical staff, held back asking if I was in need of further assistance. I knew I looked bad (and felt worse) but there was no way I was going to throw the towel in at this point. My legs still felt fresh. It was merely some stomach issues holding me back. I had 30 hours to finish the race and with 38 miles complete, I had only used 6.5 hours of my allotted time.

My new reality led me to alter my original plan. Taking the advice of the medical staff, I sipped two cups of ginger ale. However, I ignored their next piece of advice, which consisted of having me sit down and relax. I knew better than to get comfortable at any time during my 100 miles. Had I wanted comfort, I would have run home and slept on my own couch. One of the first pieces of advice I heard when I started racing ultras was "beware of the chair." It was common knowledge that sitting down and getting comfortable after being out on the course will make a runner think twice about heading back out.

Seeing my distress, my friend Jeremy played his best social worker role, telling me how bad I looked and that he didn't see any way I could continue. He was joking and thought it would get me going again, which it did. He made me laugh and I got up to head back out on the trail. I left the aid station in great spirits even though I knew it was going to be tough for me to continue on in the race. My mind was in good spirits but my stomach still wasn't agreeing with me and there was no doubt a product like Desatin (to relieve diaper rash) was soon to be my best friend. Running with a painful rash can make for a miserable day of running.

Traci had everything ready for me as I made my way back to finish another loop. As a friend grabbed me a clean shirt and Traci wiped the salt off my face, I could read their looks of worry. Ignoring their concerned sideways glances to each other, I headed out quickly, determined not to think about how bad the previous loop had been. Rather, I focused my intentions on looking for friends coming from the other direction to boost my spirits. One by one, we passed each other. I could see that they could tell I was not doing well. While my stomach was starting to feel better, I couldn't establish any kind of running rhythm.

The aid station volunteers once again proved the support of the ultra-running community. Whether it was out of pity or truth, the aid station captain reminded me, "You're the local on the course; we all have your back, and you're moving great. Now get in there and pick up your pacer." Using his words as motivation, I picked up my knees and flew from that point. With about a half-mile to go, I saw my coach John and his son out cheering me on. After a briefing on nutrition, pace and tempo, I finished 100K (62.6 miles) in 15th place.

Greeted by my familiar bright yellow McDowell Mountain Man shirt, I found my pacer, Deb, ready to tackle the next loop of the course together. As a courtesy to Traci and my crew, I had adopted yellow as my race color of choice. Very few runners wear yellow and it made it very easy for her to spot me from the aid stations. I had made several shirts for my crew, pacers, and friends to give myself a welcome sign as I ran into the aid stations.

Simply knowing I would have someone to talk to about the highs and lows of the day was comforting to me. In our conversations, I was reminded that it was football Saturday back in my home state of Michigan. I usually watched every game and there was one going on right then. I wasn't sure if knowing the score would help settle my mind or make me tenser, but ever the vigilant friend and pacer, Deb found me a score. The first update came at mile 6 in the loop – Michigan by 10 with four minutes left in the game. She didn't need to say anything else to get me motivated. We took a few small walk breaks on the hills but we continued on at a swift pace. Moving well on the downhill, I knew my stomach was still in need of repair. I sent Deb ahead to the aid station to refill my bottles while I used the bathroom. Luckily, I was in and out, feeling better than I had in hours. I yelled back to the aid station that runner 23 was leaving but Deb didn't hear me, nor did the volunteers. Instead, I unintentionally dropped the pacer I had looked so forward to picking up for the first 10.5 hours of the race. Despite feeling like I was running with the wind at my back, it did not take long for Deb to catch me.

After finishing the loop, it was nice to get some quick sugar into the system to keep the adrenaline flowing. Deb briefed my next pacer, JT, on how I was feeling, where I was struggling, and pacing. Inexperienced in trail running and pacing, JT never showed any signs of weakness. While I had previously run with JT a few times during group runs, I did not know much of his story.

As we heard the distant crowd cheer for the race winner, JT shared that his dad had passed at 57. I could tell right away just how much his dad had meant to him as he knew what my dad meant to me. The mental relief JT gave me not only by being there, but also by allowing me to talk about the man who started me on this crazy journey, propelled us to mile 87. I told JT I was going to run in front since my legs felt light. We hammered through the rocky section and he encouraged me the whole way, telling me how well I was running, how proud my dad would be, and just how amazed he was that someone could run like that after 87 miles.

At mile 88 the inevitable happened, and I tripped and fell. Surprise, surprise, surprise--it was a flat, smooth section. That seemed almost as dumb as running by the aid station in the first loop.

When I completed the sixth loop, I was given a glow necklace to signify I was on my last loop. Runners coming from the other direction saw my necklace and cheered me on. With an extra glow, I picked up my friend Tere who had paced me during my first ultra and three months prior at the Lean Horse 100, determined to keep a nine- to 10-minute pace and finish the race strong. She did not allow excuses and repeated her motto, "I know it hurts; it is supposed to hurt. If it didn't hurt that would mean you're not running hard enough."

We approached the two-mile aid station and I received huge cheers from the volunteers, who told me what place I was now in and not to let up. I didn't have much energy for the uphill and my legs were tired, so Tere and I walk/ran until we got to the flat section. I could see the final aid station off in the distance and from that point on I knew it was all downhill back to the finish. Even the downhill is tough when you're tired and have 99 miles on your legs, but I just kept talking to T in my head and he pushed me along. Farther and farther down the hill we went until we hit the sign that said 1.04 miles to go. My watch was now reading over 100 miles finished and I had just run my longest distance ever. In my typical fashion, I had to stop, gather myself and fight back the tears. As I made my way to the finish line I kept saying, "This run was for you, T." I could feel his presence with me. While I would have loved to have him physically there running beside me, I knew he was there in spirit and he was not going to let me take my foot off the gas. I crossed the road and in my typical fashion I let out a loud "Hell yeah!" to let Traci know I was on my way in. I yelled loud for that last section and crossed the finish line in 18:28:12. This was good enough for ninth place overall and a 33-minute Personal Record in the 100-mile distance.

I did finish after midnight, but the miles I had run from midnight on did not total four. So, in order for the streak to continue I would need to run an additional 1.53 miles sometime the next afternoon. I had started to hear whispers from people saying to just stop the streak, and you will run faster. Maybe so, but that wasn't my main goal. I wasn't running to be faster, smoother, or to win tons of races. I was running for my dad. People outside my running circle saw the streak as narcissistic, but many of them didn't know the real reason I had started. I guess I could have stopped and explained to everyone why I was running, but I didn't feel it necessary. This was between me and my dad and I didn't mind keeping it that way. Sure, I'd tell my close friends and those who really wanted to know; but whenever I encountered an individual who clearly didn't support the idea of my running every day I would smile, say "Thanks for the concern," and move on.

I knew I would always have Traci's support. Without fail, she shows up at all of my ultra-races. She waits for hours to see me only for a few minutes. She puts up with me every morning at 3 am when I crawl out of bed to get my run in. I try to be quiet, but I know it wakes her and she never complains. She understands me and understood my reasons for starting the streak.

Chapter 22: Failure After Failure

It took several failed attempts and even an initial rejection before I met my beautiful wife, Traci.

My first dating attempt started at the Country Club where I worked during the summer. I met a girl who started working there not long after me, and while she didn't attend school with me she did live in the same apartment complex. She had a boyfriend at the time but he worked nights and was rarely around during the day. She mentioned a few times that she'd been trying to end it with him for quite a while, which gave me the impression that their relationship was not very serious. As I got to know her better, I was convinced that our relationship would be perfect. I couldn't wait for theirs to be over so our relationship could begin.

I had no intention of sharing her with someone else but months passed by and she still hadn't broken up with her boyfriend. She would tell me all the time how boring he was and how he didn't enjoy any of the same activities that she participated in. She hung out with me almost every night and never seemed concerned about getting back home to see him. I'd hear her telling him over the phone where she was and who she was with and not once did I ever hear her lie to him about it.

Time kept passing by and I started getting jealous. She was with him each day and with me at night. It was easy for me not to think about it when I was at work, but when we were together, my thoughts would wander. I knew my anxiety would get the best of me eventually and a few months later I finally reached my boiling point.

By this time he had also had enough of her indecision and asked her to choose which one of us she was going to stop seeing. After everything I'd heard about this guy, there was no doubt in my mind that he'd be the one she would let go.

I guess I was naïve to think that she'd choose to stay with me over him but apparently he made a very good living and was paying most of her bills which meant it was the end of the road for the two of us. At first I just attributed the bags of new clothing and the way she always talked about material possessions to her upbringing. I told myself that she must have come from a wealthy background and convinced myself that it was nice that she was able to have the things she wanted. I just didn't realize at the time how far off I was from fitting into that plan. My initial reaction was to be angry about the whole situation, but as time went on I quickly realized that she was living a double life and it was something I didn't want to play any part in.

***

A couple months had gone by and I began to move on and go on the occasional date but I never found anything serious or anyone who really caught my attention. I met a few girls at parties who seemed to have interest in me but they weren't my type, and besides, I had just gotten out of a weird relationship. My friends and roommates encouraged me to move on and find someone else but I wasn't ready for anything.

I really wanted to find someone that I could spend more time with, but with everyone I met I put up a defense mechanism. It became harder and harder to trust girls I met. I could only see the negative in everyone and I started to become depressed. I looked at my brother Bryan and thought, Why can't I find a good girl like he's found? I always found it strange that I was looking for the same thing he and his friends had with their current girlfriends but at the same time I always wondered if they were really happy. Did they get tied down too quickly? Were these really the girls for them or had they not had a chance to go out and find the one?

I started working at a local video store to try and earn some extra money on the weekends. Within a few weeks I had my eye on a pretty co-worker. She was about the same age as me and she seemed exceptionally nice. She wasn't attending college at the time and had no desire to get a degree, but there was something about her that drew me in. As I got to know her better, I discovered something I had never seen before. At work she was so sweet and innocent, but outside of work she was a party girl who lived with her mom and had little to no concept of the word responsibility. When I met her I was blown away by how beautiful she was, but the lack of manners and respect she showed towards others after hours changed the way I saw her entirely.

My family and friends immediately expressed their concern and warned me that this was not the one. But as happens many times, in this case, love was blind and I ignored them. I was convinced that I'd be the one to change this girl.

Within a few weeks I started discovering items missing from my apartment. My roommates eventually told me that they didn't want her there unless they were home because they suspected she was stealing. When my money started to disappear, I finally realized I needed to confront her. While she never confessed to taking anything from me, I knew that if I had to ask, then I couldn't trust her, and if I couldn't trust her, it was time to move on.

I left the job at the video store so I could be away from her for good. She continued to call and show up at my apartment unannounced, so moving in with my brother on campus at Eastern Michigan University seemed like the obvious choice for me at the time.

***

After two failed attempts, I vowed that it would be a while before I would look for another serious girlfriend. I spent the next couple months trying to concentrate on schoolwork and decided to just have fun with my friends. One evening during a party at our apartment, I began talking to another girl and my vow to not date was broken.

This girl was attractive, had a great personality and loved sports. The only thing I could find wrong with her was she was two years older than me. I felt she was easy to talk to and we seemed to be having a great time together, but my last two relationships had left me skeptical. I started to ask probing questions to find out what was wrong with this one.

Through my line of questioning, I found out that she was a waitress. I decided that one of the best ways to get to know her would be to go up and sit in her section at the restaurant with some friends and see if her outside personality matched her work personality. She passed that test and although I moved slowly, she seemed to be very interested in me and we started a relationship.

Her interest in me soon turned to possessiveness. She would

question when I wouldn't invite her out with my friends, but there was a double standard when it came to her friends. I knew all of her friends from the numerous times we had met, but it seemed like her friends and I never got along. Since she was a couple years older than me and at the time I wasn't 21, she often frequented the bars without me. This was a tough scenario for me because I was coming off a couple dicey relationships and often wondered what was really going on at the bar when she was out until 2 am. When she was out at the bar I was supposed to accept the situation, but when I was out with my friends she didn't approve.

That summer she started working at a golf course as a cart girl and within weeks our relationship began to change. The possessive nature of previous phone calls turned to repeated arguments. I had been down this road in a previous relationship and I was getting the feeling that there was someone else. She began to call less often and several times she would pick up shifts even though she would complain to me about the treatment at work from the golfers.

As the months went by we began to grow apart and I started to wonder what I was doing with her. She wasn't that interested in dating me and I was losing interest in her. We would have conversations about splitting up and going our separate ways but she never wanted to, so I remained faithful to her. We had been dating for nine months or so and it wasn't going anywhere and the writing was on the wall that it needed to end. Going to see her seemed different and it wasn't long before she told me that she had been seeing a guy at her work.

While I was a little shocked that our relationship was over, I also had an overwhelming feeling of relief because it just so happened that I had met an amazing girl through my brother's fraternity that I couldn't get out of my mind. Although I had gone through a few failed attempts at a lasting relationship, somehow I knew that this new girl could be the one. This made our separation much more amicable since I was ready to move on.

Chapter 23: The Small-Town Girl From Ohio

When I was in my twenties, I met Traci Collyer at Eastern Michigan University in a small town called Ypsilanti, Michigan just about 10 miles outside of Ann Arbor. She was a freshman and I was a sophomore transfer from the local community college. I had no idea what I wanted to do with my life but after seeing her at a fraternity party, what I did know was that I wanted to get to know her better.

There was only one problem that was staring me right in the face: she was clearly taken and didn't really have much interest in me. It wasn't anything she said that made me feel this way; it was what she didn't say. She really didn't have anything to say to me. Maybe it was because I wasn't actually in the fraternity. Or maybe it was because she was friends with my older brother Bryan and just saw me as his little brother. Whatever it was, it bothered me. So I waited around until I could get a chance to talk to her. Towards the end of the night we spoke briefly in our "overserved" states of mind. But, even with a couple of wine coolers in her, she still had very little interest in the shaved-headed kid with baggy clothes. She wasn't mean, but she wasn't exactly going out of her way to make a connection with me. I didn't understand. Typical college kid mentality: I was a little cocky, thought I was cooler than I was, and even wondered how she could possibly be with her current boyfriend over me.

I can now chalk that up to being young and dumb but I thought this was just how everyone was in college. Boy chases after girl, boy impresses girl, girl leaves old boyfriend and finds interest in the new guy. Not quite the case and I could see this was not going to be easy, but I wasn't going to give up trying.

Weeks went by and I hadn't bumped into Traci anywhere on campus. Because I knew she hung out with my brother from time to time, I basically became a fixture at the Phi Sigma Kappa house where he was a fraternity member. Her sorority was the sister house for the Phi Sigma Kappa house so most events involved both groups. Hanging out there would ensure that I would eventually cross paths with her again soon.

I never saw the point in joining the fraternity. It cost money to be part of the group and I was already playing on all of their intramural sports teams and attending every function, even though I wasn't technically a member. I guess you could say I was an honorary member. The only events I couldn't attend were the formals, but this didn't bother me because I really had no interest in attending. They would get all dressed up a couple times a year and take their current girlfriends out for a fancy dinner and dancing and I saw that as too much work. Why couldn't we just go down to the local bar and hang out or go to a party? Besides, we had our whole lives to grow up and be adults.

What I neglected to realize was that was exactly what the girls from the sorority house wanted to do. That is what Traci wanted to do. They grew tired of the same old parties and bar scene and wanted different things in their lives. Spending time with their boyfriends at fancy events like that gave them hope and perhaps an indication of how good the future could be.

I always wanted to find the right person and eventually settle down, but I saw no point in doing things too quickly. What if I made a rash decision and settled down with the wrong person? I wanted to be married only once and have as good as a relationship with my wife as my parents had together. By that time they had been married for 27 years and always seemed so happy.

My brother was the opposite. He always seemed to be tied down in long-term relationships and while it seemed like he was happy, I never was quite sure if he truly was or if it was actually just an act. I got to see his relationships play out when I moved in with him and his roommate Scott. Bryan and Scott had lived together for a few years and were fraternity brothers at Phi Sigma Kappa. Scott was very similar to Bryan with the long-term relationships and I just never understood how they could get so involved with someone so early in life. It wasn't until Traci walked into my life that my feelings about getting involved started to change.

The following semester I continued to occasionally run into Traci around campus. Each time I took a few minutes to talk to her and try to win her over. It never seemed to work. Our conversations were always short and were usually interrupted when her boyfriend would show up. I couldn't figure out why Traci was with him. They were polar opposites. He was so self -centered and cocky. She was sweet and innocent. Whenever he was in a group, he bragged about his Beamer, talked about how wealthy his family was or pointed out the great job opportunity he had waiting for him in Chicago which would start after graduation. Traci never put herself above others. Instead, she would make a point to ask others about themselves. I knew Traci liked this guy but everything in me wanted to scream, "You are with the wrong guy!" What bothered me most was that I noticed that he would talk down to Traci as if she was somehow beneath him. Didn't he know how amazing Traci was? Didn't he realize what he had? I would never do that to her and I was going to do everything in my power to show her that I was the guy for her.

For the rest of the school year, I kept trying to convince Traci to leave her boyfriend, but it didn't seem to work. I also started to lose interest in what I was studying. I knew that I could eventually use a business degree later in life but it just didn't interest me.

With only two years left in college, I started to think about the career I would like to have when I graduated. I had always had a strong work ethic. I made pizzas, bussed tables, served food, worked at Subway making sandwiches, but the restaurant industry was not for me. I worked at a movie store for a while but that didn't interest me either. Finally, I found something I enjoyed when on the grounds crew at a local country club. I had previous experience working at a small golf club by my house the summer after I graduated high school and then I had switched courses to the local club when I found out there were opportunities for advancement. Back then I wasn't looking for a career but I enjoyed what I did and there was definitely some money that could be made in the golf course management industry. I also liked the idea that with this career I could move to another state and work year-round on golf courses. If something better came up I would be open to it, but maybe this was what I wanted to do.

During my third year at the club I learned something very interesting from my boss. He was the golf course superintendent and he had gone to school for agronomy. For the first couple years I worked there, I had assumed that he had just worked his way from the ground up and had become the superintendent. As we drove around the golf course that day I asked him many questions about his career: What exactly is an agronomist? You studied grass in school? What kind of classes do you have to take? Is it an associate's degree or do you have a bachelor's in general studies with a minor in turf grass? We talked for hours that day and one of the things he told me that stuck in my mind was that whatever you choose to do with your life in school, it is most likely how you will spend the next 40 years. I started to think about the degree I had been working towards and the thought of working in a generic business field for the rest of my life bothered me. I wanted to be outdoors, and being an agronomist provided this opportunity. I went home that evening and gave T a call and started to tell him what I had learned. I told him I was interested in switching majors and becoming an agronomist. I had already been going to school for a few years and since my parents were paying for my schooling I figured I should get their blessing before making the switch. I was worried they might frown upon the idea of adding more schooling when I was so close to finishing.

To my surprise, they actually thought the idea was a great one and were happy I had found something that I was passionate about. They asked me to do further research on the subject to find out what job prospects might be available for me when I graduated with such a degree. They were always very reasonable people but they wanted to make sure I was making the best choice possible. I could easily have found myself struggling through a major that I would have no interest in five years down the road and possibly one that was a dead end.

Since I wasn't too handy on the computer back then and the Internet was just a few years old, I had my brother help me explore what I could do with a degree in agronomy and where I could possibly go to get one. My mind immediately went to every university that was in a warm section of the country and in no time I had my mind set on the Arizona desert. I had never been to the desert and really didn't know anyone who had ever been there but I really liked the idea of traveling to the University of Arizona in Tucson.

After looking into it, I learned that the University of Arizona turf program only had 20 students. This paled in comparison to Michigan State University which had 500 students in their program. Everything I read said Michigan State was one of the best in the nation for agronomy and it was right in my backyard, basically. The problem was, I had grown up watching University of Michigan football games with my dad and I despised the idea of attending the rival school.

I knew it would be hard to sell the idea of moving across the country to go to school to my parents when this school was so close, but I really wanted a change in my life. Some of the bad decisions I had made in high school seemed to follow me around like a shadow and I loved the idea of starting over new in a different state.

Another big problem was the cost of attending U of A. It had one of the highest out-of-state tuitions, which would mean more money my parents would have to spend if they were going to help me out. I looked into Clemson University as well and it was a bit cheaper, so my idea was to present both options to my parents. I also promised them that I would work a part-time job on a golf course in whichever state I ended up choosing. That way I could help pay for the tuition.

Still, when we ran the numbers and determined costs of each school, it was clear that out-of-state was significantly more than Michigan State. There had to be another way. Since I was stubborn about not attending that school, my brother and I searched the Internet again for more options. After hours of searching, my brother found a little school in Phoenix, Arizona called the Mundus Institute. This wasn't a school where I was going to earn a bachelor's degree or even an associate's degree, but I would be able to spend an entire semester solely studying turfgrass management. With a certificate in turfgrass management I would be on my way to a career as an agronomist. This was significantly cheaper than a big university, but to add to the savings, I thought I could convince a few friends of mine who worked on the golf course with me to attend with me. We could share living expenses and help each other study. Since it was only going to be one semester, I looked at this opportunity as a way to get away and see if this was actually what I wanted to do with my life.

I told my friends of the idea and waited for a few weeks to see if they were interested. It was summertime, so we had a little time to decide. In the meantime, I wondered what moving might mean for my chances with Traci. I learned that, just as I was deciding whether or not to take off to Arizona, she had broken up with her boyfriend. This meant I had a chance! I would have to hurry if we were going to hit it off before I had to leave. We became better friends that summer and spent a lot of time talking at parties and various events. Even so, she seemed to keep her distance until the day I told her I was going to be moving to Arizona at the end of the summer. I don't think it surprised her that I wanted a change of scenery, but I think she was pretty surprised that I had chosen to move across the country and start over. I was happy to see that she showed any emotion after hearing I was going to leave. I thought, "This might mean she cares..." Although, it must have been the way I told her I was leaving because she seemed to get angry with me. Another opportunity ruined.

One of the last days that summer my roommate Scott and I went over to hang out with Traci and her roommate. This was going to be my last opportunity to talk with her before leaving. I thought if the moment struck me right then I would probably tell her how much I had tried over the last year to make something work, even though it was clear she had no desire. We had a few drinks, which increased my level of courage, so I told her.

I have always been a very blunt person and while I'm not exactly sure what I said to her that night (maybe I had one too many beers) I did not get the outcome I expected. Instead, she told me she never wanted to talk to me again. I had blown it. All hope for a future with Traci was over for me that night. At least it made going to Arizona a little easier. Sometimes things in life don't always work out as you expect them to. It didn't work out for me and Traci that night, but down the road I would get another chance.

Chapter 24: Looking to Call the Desert Home

I left in late August and headed toward the Sonoran desert. I was dying to meet some new friends and start the next chapter in my life. Three of us moved to Arizona and shared a place in Scottsdale not far from where I live today. None of us had any idea about Arizona except that it was hot and seemed like the perfect place to be. When we arrived, it far exceeded our expectations and the young, vibrant feel of the city made us come alive and think just how much we had missed out on back in the cold weather state of Michigan.

After a few weeks there I loved it. I really had no plans on returning to Michigan, even though I had told my parents the semester in Arizona would be a trial period to see if I wanted to continue studying there. No part of me liked the idea of leaving the beautiful sunshine and going back to the cold. I had spent the first 21 years of my life in the cold and I was sick of it. I dreaded winter each year and its yearly arrival meant I didn't have any work at the golf course and would have to seek out tedious part-time jobs. It never snows in Phoenix. I immediately felt like it was my new home.

Any time you move to a new place it is scary, but at the same time you know that every day you will get to experience something you hadn't seen the previous day. I grew tired of Michigan and I really just needed to try something new and exciting. Sometimes you find yourself in a rut and the only way to get out is to completely make a change, and this was no different. I had a great family and would miss them very much. In the back of my mind was always a plan to convince the family to move out west too.

The first month went so quickly and we were spending eight hours a day in the classroom studying turfgrass. It was exposing me to a side of the business I hadn't even known existed. Turfgrass management was not just growing grass; it was the science behind it, the business side of maintaining a staff and budget, water quality, chemistry, and horticulture. Obviously I knew that the business was much more than sending a few guys out each day to mow fairways and greens, but what I didn't know was the amount of chemistry and knowledge that was required to maintain a healthy balance in the turf grass plant. We spent weeks on fertilizers, chemicals, soils, and irrigation. After half the semester I was content with the path I had chosen. I no longer had any ambition to go to school to be a businessman; I wanted to be a golf course superintendent no matter what it took.

It seemed as though the teachers and other professionals in the field would try to scare us with the amount of hours required each day in order to make this a profession but that was neither here nor there. I loved the sheer beauty of the golf course, loved working with different people, and there was nothing better than spending 10 to 12 hours every day, driving around a golf course making it look perfect. I always found it extremely rewarding to see a project through from beginning to end. This might be an inherited quality because my dad never gave up on a project and often took over projects for others, satisfying a need for perfection. Since I'm far from handy, this was a way for me to showcase my skills and see a finished project seven days a week.

As Thanksgiving approached, I knew I was going to have to make a quick decision about which school I would attend for the second semester. My mom and dad would be asking what I had decided on when I visited them for the holidays. I had received my acceptance letter to the University of Arizona, and one to Clemson University; as a favor to my parents, I had also applied to the local school, Michigan State University, and was accepted. I really wasn't even considering MSU but part of me worried about starting over again in Tucson. This time I was going to have to do it alone because my friends would be moving back to attend Michigan State so they could get in-state tuition. You needed to be a resident for a year before receiving in-state tuition in Arizona but I would need to take the second semester off in order to make that happen. This really seemed like the best approach and plan. Although I did worry that now I was going to be on my own and I might get lonely. If the turf program was as small as I had read about at the time, it was unlikely I would get to meet many people, especially living off campus.

Days went by and I kept pondering the decision but nothing seemed to make sense except sucking it up and moving back to attend

Michigan State. I thought about money, jobs, friends, quality of education. I also thought about Traci. Yes, she had told me she never wanted to see me again the last time I saw her in Michigan... but I still thought I had a chance. I figured both of us would have changed over the months I had been away. Besides, how long could she hold a grudge against me? I was hoping by now she had realized that whatever I had said or done that night was just a drunken mistake.

Chapter 25: A Return to the Cold

Deciding to come back to Michigan was no easy task, especially since I had sold most of my stuff in Michigan and I was going to have to make the cross-country drive back, which only months before, I had sworn I would never do again. The drive to Arizona the first time felt like it took a week, even though it was only two and a half days. I was young and had no patience, so sitting in a jam-packed Chevrolet Cavalier didn't exactly suit me.

Since T was happy with my decision to leave Arizona and attend Michigan State where I could get in-state tuition, he agreed to fly out and make the drive back to Michigan with me. Not exactly the best vacation days he ever took, but he was truly excited about me coming back close to home and he had no issue making the 30-hour drive to Michigan with me. He saw it as a way to catch up and bond like we used to. I was glad I wasn't going to have to make the drive back alone and if I was going to be in a car for 30 hours, there was no better person to keep me entertained. We never seemed to grow tired of each other and he accepted me exactly as I was, flaws and all.

He was always a forward thinker and would remind me that I had a bright future in store for me if I played my cards right. I might have had trouble early on in life but he looked at those times as positive learning experiences. He told me people don't discover their true character until years down the road, when it might be too late. but that I had had the opportunity to overcome some tough situations and find mine early on.

The ride back was pretty uneventful, with a stop in Albuquerque to spend the night and a lovely stop at the riverboat casino in East St. Louis. Yes, the East St. Louis that is made so famous by the scene in *National Lampoon's Vacation*. It had that strange Detroit vibe where you don't worry about what you see and hear; you worry about what you're not seeing. The streets seemed like ghost towns and no one stopped at the traffic lights, giving you the feeling that at any moment your life could take an unexpected turn.

We spent a few hours out on the riverboat playing blackjack, and the good times seemed to roll as we were winning and making money. I didn't have much money then, since I wasn't working, but T had given me a couple hundred dollars to play. The general rule of thumb in cards is to "know when to walk away," but our cards just kept coming up aces. We set the amount at $500 to walk away or if we hit a little losing streak that would take our profits below $200, but that never happened. Within minutes we were up $500 each and walking out the casino door all smiles.

The good news was that we were in East St. Louis and there was nowhere we were going to spend any money, but the bad news was we were going to have to get back in the car and continue on to Chicago. We could have taken a quicker route, but I hadn't seen my cousin in a while and it made for a good stop before we would head back to Michigan. Seeing family again lifted my spirits, but the Chicago lake-effect winds greeted us, leaving me to question my decision to move back to Michigan.

It was great to get home and see family in Michigan, but I was still confused about what I wanted to do for school. I knew Michigan State would be my best option but since I had missed the first semester and it was tough to start in the middle of the year, I figured I would knock out 15 additional credits at Washtenaw Community College. I had been living on my own since I was 18, and the 30-minute commute from my parents' house to Washtenaw Community College led me to look for a better living arrangement.

Bryan and Scott lived close to Washtenaw and offered to let me crash on the couch until I figured out a plan. What they didn't know was the plan wouldn't be finalized until six months down the road. I bought a futon for a couch (and a bed!) and decided I would make myself comfortable as long as I could. The place was a small two-bedroom apartment but they didn't seem to mind having me around.

Scott spent most days away at his girlfriend's house so we had a little extra room at the place, but living on a futon in my brother's apartment and attending community college didn't exactly make me a chick magnet. "Hey, do you want to come over and hang out on my futon?" "Don't mind the other people here, I live in the living room and my clothes are in the coat closet." It is a running joke between my brother, Scott, and me now but it sure wasn't funny at the time. Bryan and I always got along really well so I never felt uncomfortable living at his place--until the great grill incident of 1998.

My boss had just purchased a new propane grill and he wanted to know if we would like to take his old one. Being 21 years old and poor, I was happy to take it off his hands. Besides, we didn't have a grill at our apartment or anywhere in the complex to use. I knew they were allowed because several of the neighbors had them on their porches and Bryan said to bring it home if it looked okay. The grill looked nice and appeared to be in good shape, plus he gave us a brand-new propane tank. I couldn't possibly turn it down and it was going to make cooking much easier for me.

I stopped at the store and picked up some hamburgers and beers. This was going to be a nice relaxing day after work. We quickly set up the grill outside and it fired up right away. I walked back into the house while the lid was down and the grill was heating. I was only inside for a few seconds when I looked out the window to see smoke and fire!

Bryan and I rushed outside to see what was going on. The propane tank was completely engulfed in flames. Living on the second floor, it would take only seconds for the fire to get out of control. The porch had a wood deck; I knew it was only a matter of time before the fire crept to the building. I was freaking out at the thought of the whole building catching on fire.

I quickly grabbed baking soda, thinking it would help, but this was like bringing a knife to a gun fight. The flames doubled in size and the only option was to call the fire department.

Thank God we lived close to a fire station. Within seconds we could hear the sirens screaming and the police cars pulling into the parking lot. I was banging on the neighbors' doors, telling them to get out of the building. All I could think was, my only addition to the apartment was going to bring the whole building down. The guy living on the couch had set the building on fire.

It was an embarrassing scene, trying to tell other residents that all of their possessions might be gone in the next few minutes and to grab their animals and get out of the building. The fire department arrived, and as they made their way to the back of the building they realized they would have to move quickly to prevent the entire building from catching on fire A few firemen ran up the stairs and with a high-powered fire extinguisher they put out the flames. Thankfully, this was just in time before the rest of the building caught on fire, but not in time to clear me of a level of embarrassment I would never live down.

I had cleared out an entire apartment complex and I was probably the most hated person in the building. Luckily, my brother's lease was coming to an end, so the evil stares from neighbors only lasted a few more weeks. After that fateful day I made the final decision to attend Michigan State University in the fall.

Chapter 26: Aligning With a Rival

My first day in East Lansing was interesting. I moved my stuff into the four-bedroom dump we called a house on Gunson Street with seven roommates. The house was zoned for five people but there was a finished basement for my friend Will, leaving me with my own room on the main floor. There were three girls who lived upstairs and four guys who lived downstairs. That was Monday through Thursday, and the weekends always seemed to bring about three or four more people to our house, so it was a tight squeeze.

Gunson Street was well known as one of the biggest party streets on campus and no one at our house seemed to take that honor lightly. We wanted to keep up with the Joneses so we seemed to have a party going at least four times a week. Quiet time was a luxury that really only happened between 9 am and 3 pm, when everyone was supposed to be at class.

My roommate Will and I were turfgrass majors, so our lives consisted of chemistry, biology, math, and soil science. It would be hard for me to explain just how tiring these classes were to attend, especially after a long night of drinking. We would attend classes with pre-med students and chemistry majors, hoping the curve for the class wouldn't be set too high. Ideally you would see a curve that ranged from 35 percent being passing to 80 percent being an A. Most of the time that was pretty typical, but there were a few pathology classes where the curve would be set so high that we had no choice but to hit the books and actually study during the week.

I was interested in any topics having to do with turfgrass, but when it came to chemistry classes I just couldn't keep focused and couldn't see the reason for learning the material. I wondered when I would ever use this stuff. (I've come to find out: chemistry has become a part of my job daily, so I really should have listened back then. Because I only paid enough attention to squeak by in chemistry class and it ended up being such a large part of my career, I was later forced to retake classes and actually learn much of the material well after receiving my degree.)

By the second semester of school I was ready to leave East

Lansing and return to living in Ann Arbor. I had met a lot of great friends but I still missed my friends from home and thought if I was going to live in Michigan I should at least be closer to friends and family. My roommates and I discussed the next year's living situation and since most places didn't accept more than five people in a house, I volunteered to move out to make it easier for them. They all had a couple years of school to go and I only had my senior year.

Living in Ann Arbor, I could work at the golf course on days I didn't have classes. It wasn't that far of a drive for me and I only had a few months left in school, so my moving out seemed like the obvious choice.

The next month after finals I made it official that I was going to move back to my parents' house for the summer. While there, I would look for a place of my own somewhere between Ann Arbor and East Lansing, with hopes of moving there in the fall.

Going home that May was rewarding and difficult at the same time. I once again felt the need to live on my own, since I had been doing so since I was 18, but I wasn't quite sure where I wanted to go. T said it would be just as easy to live at home as it would be to find a place to live.

Chapter 27: Learning When to Stay or Walk Away

Before my senior year at Michigan State University, my summer plan was not only to make good money while working at the country club, but also to use my skills at the blackjack table and try to increase my take-home. While this was far from a good idea on my small income, I had been working on my card-counting skills since taking a course at Michigan State on gaming.

I had a professor who was a professional blackjack player and after class we would run through different techniques. This wasn't a blackjack club or anything that you would see in the movies, just a professor who was looking for a couple students to share his knowledge and love of the card game. I loved the game of blackjack and while I had read many books on card counting it never seemed to register with me. I had assumed you needed to be an MIT student or something similar to pick up the concept, but for two days a week after class for the semester I had worked on mastering the game of blackjack. We walked through so many scenarios about where to sit, what to look for, and how to maximize your dollars, but I assumed all this was irrelevant since I was making $18,000 a year at my current job. No one in their right mind should go out and try to increase their income when living at or below the poverty line, but my addictive personality took over again.

I figured the summer was as good of a time as any to hone my blackjack skills since I was living at home and if it didn't work out then, worst case scenario, I would probably have to continue living at home for the school year. I had some extra time on my hands and honing my blackjack skills also helped teach me about patience. There was a skill to card counting but waiting for the right cards and count to develop sometimes took hours. I had to learn to accept that I wasn't just going to sit down at a table and instantly make money.

T was behind my newfound interest in blackjack and he knew I loved playing. He even took my brother and me to Vegas for my 21st birthday. I told him I was learning to count cards and while it was no exact science I felt I had a pretty good grasp of the game to put the odds in the player's favor. Now there are circumstances that could easily flip things upside down and the biggest variable when playing is the players around you, but I felt comfortable with my odds. I would always look for a table with consistent play and while it didn't really matter if they were hitting or staying at the appropriate times, what mattered was that they stayed consistent from hand to hand. Once you had a good read of a table, the next step was to wait for the first seat to open up. Sometimes this would involve walking between tables for an hour but eventually you would find the right fit to try and make a move.

The first night that my dad and I went to the downtown Detroit casinos I went with just a few hundred dollars and my plan was to play low-dollar tables and just work on my technique in a live game. I had been running through the decks of cards so many times at home and I was ready to challenge myself.

While you're not able to tell the exact card that the dealer might hand you, the odds would tell you whether the card was going to be a 2–6, 7–9 or 10–ace. I used the same techniques that made the students from MIT famous, but at that time I had never heard of them or read the book *Bringing Down the House*. The casinos always operated with multiple decks, which threw a major wrench in most games, but there was always a table or two of double deck blackjack.

Sitting down at a blackjack table would give me the same high that I get today from finishing an ultra-marathon. My nerves would be going, and while most people around me were drinking cocktails and yelling at the dealer for giving them bad cards, I was busy studying all the hands around me. I would count the low cards 2–6 as +1 and the high cards 10–ace as -1, and the middle cards 7–9 had no value, so I would just gloss over those cards when I saw them.

At first I felt overwhelmed as the dealer would split the cards out across the felt table. But just like NFL quarterbacks say the game slows down once they learn the team's offence, it felt like the dealer was slowing down so I could keep track of what was going on. For the player to use the count in their favor, anything over a +5 would indicate that it was a good time to up the ante and make a run at the hand. It didn't mean you were going to win the hand but it did mean that the deck was in your favor as a player and the odds had shifted against the house.

Getting into a good positive count always got the blood flowing and I would begin to sweat a little, wondering if I really had the count right or if I had missed quite a few cards that had been dealt. T agreed ahead of time to give my technique a go and play his bets based on how I was betting. If I was raising my $10 bet to $25–$30 a hand, he would double his hand from $25 to $50.

Chapter 28: A Second Chance

One night on the drive home from the local casino, T brought up the topic of Traci. She had called the house earlier in the day and I had blown her off. I think I was mad at her for not giving me a chance or maybe I was just giving up. I soon learned the reason for her call. She wanted to know if I still had the graphing calculator she had seen me use once back when I was still attending school in Michigan. She would be taking some sort of math class during the summer semester and was trying to avoid spending the $100 to buy a new one.

I had tried for two years to get to know her better and now that I was back in Michigan visiting, all she wanted was my calculator? There were hundreds of people she could borrow a calculator from. Why was she insistent on driving 25 minutes to borrow mine? She had been basically non-responsive to my attempts to win her over in the past so, now that she needed me for something, I wanted to be stubborn and not call her back.

My dad kept prying, asking me why I didn't just suck it up and call the girl. After all, if it was really just a calculator she wanted then her coming to pick it up would be quick and painless. But, what if it was a ploy to come see me? Part of me liked the idea that she might be using the "need for a calculator" as an excuse to come see if there was anything between us. The other part wasn't sure I could handle being shut down by this girl again if all she truly wanted was to use me for my calculator.

The next day she called again and again. I stuck to my stubbornness and refused to answer. I told my dad to tell her that I wasn't home. After a while he thought I was being foolish and wouldn't play along. He told Traci I was tied up, but he would make sure to have me call her right back. T and my mom made me feel guilty about not calling her. They convinced me to at least pick up the phone, and if I didn't want to see her, at least tell her that I didn't have a calculator she could borrow. They didn't condone lying but they also didn't want me to keep ignoring her. So I finally picked up the phone and called Traci.

I made it short and sweet. I told her she could borrow the

calculator, gave her my address and told her I might not be home when she came to pick it up, but I would leave it for her. The truth was I had nowhere to go, so of course I would be home, but the idea of seeing her walk through my front door made me nervous. I worried that all the feelings I had for her would come rushing back—they really never left. I wasn't sure how I would act when I saw her and I wanted a way out in case it was too much.

That afternoon as I was relaxing in the den and talking to T again about Traci, I looked out the window and locked eyes with Traci walking up the drive. Damn. She had seen me. Now I definitely couldn't hide. And sure enough, the moment I saw her, the feelings came rushing back. This time my heart beat even faster than the times I had seen her before. I prepared myself for what was sure to be an awkward banter between the two of us.

When she stepped in the house and we began to talk, I was surprised that our exchange was nothing like I thought it would be. We actually seemed to have chemistry this time. I even invited her to hang out and watch a movie with me and was shocked when she said yes. Even today, I'm not sure what power she has over me, but every time I see her I light up, my feelings for her grow. We watched one movie and then, as if we didn't want to leave each other, we popped in another. I can't even tell you which movies we watched because the entire time they were playing I was talking to Traci. I told her how I would be home for the summer, but would be working 70 hours a week. I also told her how I had been frequenting the casino to perfect my blackjack skills. As soon as I brought up the casino, I thought I had put my foot in my mouth. I thought, "Great! She isn't going to like a degenerate gambler." But this didn't drive her away. She actually said she would like to learn blackjack too and asked if she could go with me sometime.

I think I was so used to her shutting me down in the past that her acceptance of me this day completely threw me off. When she left that day, I agreed to take her to the casino and told her I would give her a call.

The next week I picked up Traci and we headed to the casino in Windsor, Canada. At the time the dollar was worth a $1.50 to the

Canadian dollar and just bringing a couple hundred dollars made me feel like I had more money to play with. Traci was very skeptical of gambling when we arrived, really believing we were there to "donate" our money to the casino. She did want to learn the game of blackjack, though, so that is where we started. She sat and watched me play the first few hands and when the seat next to me opened she jumped in, ready to throw down and make some money.

I told her it would be difficult to make much money because she hadn't brought very much to play with, but we would give it a try. The hands the dealer had dealt up to this point weren't generating many wins on the table, so I told her to keep her bets on the low side to start. Maybe when this set of cards ran out and the dealer reshuffled, our luck would increase. Traci was trying to figure out just how the game worked and every time the cards were dealt, I was leaning over to tell her what to do with her hand. This presented a little issue in my game play because I was struggling to pay any attention to what was going on at the rest of the table. The cards were coming out of an automatic shuffler with eight decks of cards, so any advantage I perceived myself to have wouldn't help.

I taught Traci the general rules of blackjack: which numbers to "hit" based on what the dealer showed, when to "stay," to always split aces and 8s, and double down on 11. When she got dealt a hand she wasn't sure what to do with she would look at me for reassurance. It made me feel good to know she trusted me. I would throw chips her way if she was short and also to show her that I would make the same bets I was telling her to make. Before long, Traci was up $100. I was paying little attention to what was going on at the table and a lot of attention to Traci, but I managed to keep winning too.

That evening we left the casino up $1,000 between the two of us and we were ready to celebrate. We celebrated in style with a fancy steak dinner at a restaurant most hardworking adults could only afford once every couple of years on a special occasion. To me this was a very special occasion. This was a start of a relationship with Traci that I had been working towards for a long time. Any time we had seen each other in the past was always around other people. This sit-down dinner gave us a chance to really get to know each other, just the two of us.

That night over dinner she asked what my plans were for the next year and what I was going to do with my degree once I finished my education in turfgrass management. Without even thinking before I answered, I said "The day I finish school I'm moving back to Arizona." I hadn't really thought of the consequences of this statement but I could see in her face that she didn't like hearing it. I wasn't trying to make her angry or upset. At this point I really liked her and wanted to spend all my time with her, but my heart was also set on moving back to Arizona. Again, I thought to myself "Foot in mouth! How do you always do this?" Just as I was getting ready to explain, Traci said "I would love to go to Arizona sometime." What? This was music to my ears. I was thrilled to hear her say that and in my mind I immediately started planning a trip for her to come see me in Arizona. We talked and talked that evening and before the night was over I was convinced that she was the one for me.

That summer we visited the casino so many evenings that the dealers knew our names. After a few long nights at the table, the pit bosses even "comp'd" a hotel room for us so we wouldn't have to drive home tired. I loved hanging out with Traci so much that I often found myself spending the whole night with her in Windsor before dropping her off at home at 4 am and then scrambling to get to work by 5 am. When I was in college, it was easier to rebound after such a night. The clock was irrelevant as long as I was having fun and could make it to work on time.

Gambling was so much fun, and while we would lose a lot of nights, we also won a lot of nights and it sure made the nights more exciting to get put up in a hotel suite for the evening. I wasn't winning that much money, but it was covering all our dating expenditures and we were having the time of our lives together. We began dating and I couldn't imagine finding someone more perfect. We never argued and she accepted me even with my flaws.

As the end of summer drew near I worried that our fun would come to an end. I had one more year left at Michigan State and Traci had two years remaining at Eastern Michigan, so I approached her with the idea of moving in with me and living halfway between Ann Arbor and East Lansing. I didn't think she was going to go for this idea. There wasn't much between our two schools besides a small town called Howell, Michigan. There wouldn't be much to do there and it would be away from her friends. To my surprise she was on board with the idea. We looked at a few apartments and finally decided on one we both liked. She would commute 30 minutes to school and I would commute 45 minutes each way. Sure, it was a lot of driving, but at least we would be able to see each other every day, so it was worth it. This was working out really well until Traci became sick.

I noticed her losing an extreme amount of weight and she would get excruciating pains all over her body. The doctors diagnosed her with lupus. Every week she seemed to get a little worse and the colder it grew outside, the more her body began to ache. Doctors told her she had arthritis like an 85-year-old woman and unfortunately with her lupus, she would experience these pains for the rest of her life. This was not an easy thing for her to hear.

It was hard on me to watch the girl I was falling in love with get sicker by the day. I wanted to help her and make her feel better, but nothing I did helped. They gave her so many different medications that made her tired and weak. She could no longer finish the semester at school and completely lost interest in finishing her dietetics major. On the really bad days when the pain was so intense, all she could muster was lying on a heating pad or taking a hot bath and then going to bed.

Being the positive person Traci is, she would try hard not to talk about her problems and wanted to continue to go out and have fun. But I could see it in her face when she was too sick to move, so we would just rent movies and stay home together. I couldn't handle watching her get sick and I was terrified that something might happen to the girl of my dreams. These tough times brought us even closer together.

With the help of my mom and dad and the money I saved from working the summer at the golf course, I decided to buy a ring and ask Traci to marry me. I feared the unknown about her sickness, but there was no question in my mind that she was who I would spend the rest of my life with. I didn't have a ton of money but I didn't want to go cheap on the ring. I dipped into my savings from the summer of blackjack, borrowing the rest from T so I could purchase a beautiful ring.

Since a casino was where our relationship had grown, I thought it would be nice to propose to her on a trip to Vegas. That December we booked a trip and were on our way to Las Vegas. As we arrived at the airport to leave Michigan I was a nervous wreck. I kept wondering if the metal detector would pick up the ring I was trying to hide from Traci. What if she saw me pass it through the machine? Even scarier, what if I got the ring all the way to Vegas and proposed and Traci said no? Were we going to have to break up or do people move on together even if one person is not ready to get married?

We had only been together for a short period of time, but I knew we belonged together and hoped she felt the same about me.

We managed to get through the airport with no issues. My next battle was deciding where I would propose to her. I wanted to make it perfect. I didn't want to ask in a cheesy place. I developed a plan to propose the first night after a nice dinner and a show. I wasn't quite sure where yet, but I hoped the exact time and place would come to me as the night progressed. After a great dinner and an amazing show, we walked around the Venetian Hotel and my palms were hot and sweaty. I was so nervous. I wanted the proposal to be perfect. We walked past the Gondola boat rides and I thought that might be a good place, but as we made our way to the boat you could either pay extra to ride as a couple or go with a group of four. Couple, I thought but Traci spoke up and told the man accepting our money we would ride with another couple. Well, that ruined that idea. The night came to an end and I had not asked her.

We were staying at the Paris Hotel and the next morning when I woke I went on a walk to try to find a good place. I saw so many perfect places to ask her, my favorite being the Eiffel Tower. In my mind, I pictured us taking the elevator to the top and while alone, looking out on the strip, I would pop the question. The night came, we ate dinner and I had my whole speech planned out for a proposal on the Eiffel Tower. We rode to the top and I was ready, but there were so many people around. This wasn't going to work either. Besides, what if she said no and I was left rejected 20 floors up. We would have to ride the elevator back down in an awkward silence. As we made our way back down the elevator I was kicking myself for not asking her in the tower.

There was one other place I had seen earlier so I went to plan B. This was the bridge that ran above the casino floor. This was a beautiful place and while not as memorable as the top of the tower, it could be very romantic. When we got down to the bridge and started walking around, my nerves got the best of me. I immediately became sick to my stomach, thinking about how I would ask and whether or not she would say yes. I told her I wanted to go up and lie down in the room for an hour or so before we went back out. As we walked to the room, my stomach felt better. I knew it was just anxiety, but didn't know how I would proceed.

We walked into our hotel room and within seconds it hit me that there was no better time than the present. "Just ask," I thought. So, with the Vegas strip shining in our hotel window, I got down on one knee and I asked the girl of my dreams if she would marry me. She lit up and answered with a quick yes! Oh, how I was relieved. She told me how much she loved the ring, and how she loved me even more. She said she was hoping I was going to ask her, but had no idea when or where I might ask. The 17th of December, 1999, was a special day for Traci and me. It was the start of our life together.

Back home, the doctors continued to tell Traci that the cold air was negatively affecting her arthritis and to prepare for a rough time each time the winter came. She was tired of the constant pain, and dreaded the cold. We discussed the possibility of moving to Arizona once I graduated. I would be back in the place I had fallen in love with and the warm weather could help her condition. Without ever even setting foot in the state, she made up her mind that we should go.

In March of 2001, I interviewed for a position at a country club in North Scottsdale and Traci traveled with me out to the desert. Minutes after stepping off the plane, Traci was in love with the warm weather and told me she would be very happy to move there. She was going to be starting back at school to finish her dietetics major and figured a transfer to a new school, coupled with the warmer weather, would give her a fresh start and the energy she needed to finish.

Chapter 29: A Fresh Start in Arizona

While the job I interviewed for didn't work out, I was offered a job later that summer and was told I could start in September of 2001. We were so happy to finally have the chance to move out to Arizona together and even though we were not married at the time, we lived like we had been married for years. We split everything down the middle for bills and combined our incomes just like most married couples do, even though the actual vows would not take place for another nine months.

I loved the idea of going back to Arizona but I hated the idea of being 2,000 miles away from my mom and dad again. Even though I had made times hard for them during my teenage years, they never gave up on me and our relationship was stronger than ever. T didn't want to see me go but he recognized this was where I wanted to live so I could pursue my dream in the field of golf and turf management. He also knew I had landed a job at the top golf club in all of Arizona, an opportunity I couldn't pass up.

My last day of work at Travis Pointe Country Club in Ann Arbor was a sad day, not only because I was leaving a job I really loved but also because it was the morning of September 11, 2001.

As I came in from mowing greens on my last day, the news was playing on the radio that the Twin Towers had been hit by planes and it was a terrorist act. My heart sank for the people of New York and Pennsylvania and all I could think was, how were we going to leave on a day like this? This was one of the most tragic days in American history and all everyone wanted to do was be around family, yet we were moving 2,000 miles across the country. As I arrived home that day from work, I was in such shock and it was tough to watch the moving company packing up my stuff. The movers stood around the TV and watched as the president released his statements and we all watched the news together and our minds just weren't into the move anymore. We weren't sure what to do, but at a time like this, moving just didn't seem like the right thing to do. My dad knew how much this meant to me and knew that this feeling would pass. It was clear that I needed to take advantage of this job opportunity.

The next day we drove to Ohio to Traci's parents to drop off her car so we could drive across country together. She had just bought a new car and instead of shipping it, her parents had agreed to drive it there for us. Two days in Ohio and what was supposed to be a celebration as we said goodbye to family and friends turned out to be tough since her parents were no longer able to bring her car out. This really put a damper on an already grim weekend, but we decided to leave a day early and drive separately. This was going to be a nightmare for both of us, but in three days we would be together again and it wasn't worth the anxiety of trying to work things out.

Our first two days were long and while we stopped often for our dog Oscar to get out and stretch, I couldn't help but think this was not supposed to be the way we were supposed to start our lives together. She just had a fight with her parents and now we were driving across country during a time of sadness all across the United States.

When we arrived in Scottsdale, we were so happy to finally be together and not in separate cars. We were finally home. After days of unpacking and settling in, I started my job at Desert Mountain Golf Club. A few days later, Traci was offered a job as a sales agent at the apartment complex we were living in. This was a nice little bonus since the position offered a 25 percent discount off our rent payment. This allowed us to move into one of the larger townhouses.

Our lives were swamped with work when we first arrived and even though I would spend 80-plus hours a week at work we still managed to find plenty of time to spend together each evening. It never seemed to bug her that I was at work from sun-up until sundown every day, because she was in a new place and the warm weather had her feeling better. Within months, Traci seemed to feel 100 percent better and we were just a few months away from getting married.

Before we left we had decided that we would get married at a country club in Ohio on June 1, 2002. We picked out everything for the wedding before leaving so we would not have the issue of planning a wedding from across the country.

At 6:30 pm on the first of June we were married and the future looked so promising. We had put up a front and "disliked" each other for so many years but when we finally sat down and took the time to get to know each other, we both knew we would never be with someone else again.

When you reach a certain age and have been together for a few years, people start to question you about when you're going to have kids. Traci and I always answered this question the same and we both always felt the same way on the matter. We wanted to have kids, but first we needed to spend time with each other for a few years and work on our relationship. Our relationship had been incredible since the day we started dating and we didn't want to throw any wrenches in our marriage by having a child too quickly. We were married relatively young (by today's standards) Traci at the age of 25 and I was 26 years old. Never wanting to over-extend ourselves financially, we also decided we would wait to have kids until we knew we could afford them. This meant all of our bills were paid off and we would not be living paycheck to paycheck like we had been in previous years. In order to do this, Traci wanted to pursue other options for work and I was in full agreement with this decision.

During this time Traci learned about some family health issues with her cousins back in Ohio. Her cousin had suffered a stroke in his 30s and was severely debilitated. His movement was limited and his speech was slurred, leading doctors to tell him that he would probably never be able to work again. The doctors had been trying to figure out exactly what had happened to him.

After researching family history, the doctors discovered that his brother had had his leg amputated 10 years earlier. In order to determine if something genetic was responsible for the pain, the doctors ran multiple blood tests. The results showed a clotting disorder called factor V Leiden. This disorder affects millions of Americans but most people have no idea something is wrong with them until it is too late. It is a mutation of one of the factors in the blood called factor V. This mutation increases your chance of developing abnormal blood clots, usually in your veins. Some of the symptoms are severe pain, swelling, redness, and warmth. The doctors didn't think to ask if anyone else in the family was also suffering from these symptoms. But when we heard about factor V

Leiden, Traci and I got concerned.

She had been having these symptoms off and on for a few years now. Doctors had always told her it was severe arthritis/lupus but she was never convinced they were right. This newfound knowledge created even more concern when Traci and I decided we were ready for children.

Chapter 30: Our Rock, Our Love

Two years after getting married, Traci and I decided we were ready to have kids. We decided we wanted to just let it happen when it happened, instead of putting the stress on ourselves about conceiving. If it happened, it was meant to be and if it didn't, well then, that was okay too.

A year had gone by and she had not become pregnant. While we weren't overly concerned, we did wonder how it was possible. A couple more months went by and Traci was pregnant. We were so excited. Her first doctor's visit at 10 weeks confirmed she was in fact pregnant and the baby and Traci looked healthy. Traci explained to the doctor that she had been diagnosed with lupus a few years back but that since moving to Arizona her symptoms had been very manageable, without any flare-ups. The doctors didn't seem too concerned but they did schedule a couple extra check-up appointments during the first trimester.

Two weeks later, Traci was sick again and in a lot of pain. This time the pain was not coming from her hands and feet like it had been in the past but her whole body was in pain. We called the doctor immediately and set a time to take her in that afternoon. By the time we saw the doctor, she had miscarried the baby. This was devastating news.

For weeks we wondered why and how this could happen, but the doctor assured us that it was nothing we could have controlled. Unfortunately, sometimes miscarriages just happen. The doctor explained that Traci would need to take some time to let her body heal and after a few more checkups we would be able to try again.

No mother in the world wants to hear this news and naturally Traci didn't take it lightly. She has always been a person who researches problems, and in her research she learned about miscarriages in factor V Leiden patients. While she had not been diagnosed with this mutation, she wondered if this was what had been plaguing her for some time now. Her cousins had been diagnosed and from what she had read, she was convinced she had the very same mutation.

There were very few doctors in 2005 who had heard of factor V Leiden and even fewer who had worked with patients with this mutation. Yet Traci came across a doctor in Scottsdale who specialized in clotting disorders and also was listed as one of the top doctors to see if you've had pregnancy complications. I personally thought it was a long shot since doctors had been telling her for years that she had lupus. I thought there was no way that so many doctors would have misdiagnosed Traci. Both of her cousins were smokers and this was one of the leading risk factors for patients with factor V Leiden, so I assumed smoking was the link that caused both of them to have the disorder. Traci did not give up on the idea that she thought she also had factor V. In order for this to be properly diagnosed, she would need her mom to be checked. Her mom was never checked, which made her diagnosis very difficult until the day we met her new doctor. We went in and explained her background and talked for an hour about the pregnancy and without our telling him what we thought, he said he wanted to check her for factor V Leiden. I was in shock because I had blown off her self-diagnosis.

He explained to us what happens to the body and why pregnancy can be extremely tough for women who have this condition, but that it was also very possible to have a safe pregnancy. If this was what Traci had, the doctor ensured us he would help us in any way he could.

The tests came back to reveal that Traci did in fact have this condition and she tested negative for lupus or any other autoimmune disorders. While this was a relief, it worried me she was suffering from a severe clotting disorder. She had been on birth control pills prior to us trying to have kids, something that has been linked to blood clots in thousands of women. The birth control pills were causing tiny micro clots in her body which mimicked the symptoms of lupus and other auto-immune disorders. The doctor made sure she wasn't still on any birth control and he prescribed some anti-inflammatory medicines to help with the pain. He instructed us to wait to get pregnant for a few months in order to let Traci's body fully recover and said when checkups showed she was healthy we could try again.

We followed the doctor's orders and for a few months we made sure we were safe and she didn't get pregnant. After going back for a follow-up exam, we were given the green light to begin trying again, but we weren't very sure. I was so scared about something happening to her during a pregnancy that I tried to avoid the subject at all costs. A couple more months went by and my mind became eased as Traci started feeling better and better. The new medicine she had for the pain was working.

Soon, Traci told me she was pregnant. Our first call was to her doctor to make sure we took all the right precautions moving forward. Most of the time they will schedule your first appointment at seven to 10 weeks, but the doctor wanted to see her at six weeks. He explained the protocol and difficulties that she might face but he also said that she might very well have a safe pregnancy.

After speaking with the doctor and going in for a checkup we were told that the safest thing she could do was to start administering Heparin two times daily in her stomach. The thought of having to stick needles in her stomach two times every day for the next 32 weeks made me wonder if this was meant to be or whether we were prolonging the same outcome as last time. Patients with factor V Leiden are most vulnerable during the critical first trimester of pregnancy, so the doctors want to take every precaution at this time. Traci was determined to make this work and the needles didn't seem to be an obstacle.

Yet, just three weeks after visiting the doctor, she suffered another miscarriage. This was absolutely devastating and her depression about not being able to have a baby kicked in shortly after. For months we made sure she did not get pregnant because neither one of us could go through it again.

The doctor was not ready to give up and explained it was safe to try again. This time, when she became pregnant he would increase the Heparin dose. I wasn't so sold on this and really didn't want to see Traci ever go through this again, but she was determined to have a baby. She knew it was possible and while we had had trouble twice, there was nothing to say that we couldn't have a healthy child.

As time went on and the months passed, so did our employment opportunities. I had taken a job with a grassing company out of Southern California called West Coast Turf. They offered me a position in sales, which scared me to death since I had never done sales in my life. During this time Traci was also promoted at her job to director of financial aid. While I did not know anything about sales, I was excited at the possibilities this job was going to present. I now had the opportunity to work with golf courses all over Arizona, professional sports venues like Bank One Ball Park where the Arizona Diamondbacks play, and with landscapers on multi-million-dollar homes. My job was not to sell the product to them, but instead to explain the best grass choice for their project and help them make an executive decision. Landscape companies would call me out for my expertise on grass and ask for my opinions. Within months I had built a huge clientele. I wasn't selling them on grass but instead I was sharing my knowledge of the industry with them. Soon I was selling more grass than we could grow at our sod farm. Business went from good to great and our yearly sales doubled from one year to the next. I was starting to get the hang of sales and I also learned exactly what my customers were looking for.

As the business began to grow and Traci began to move up the ranks of her company, we made the conscious decision to try again to have a baby. Her doctor told her to let him know as soon as she was pregnant and at six weeks she called him to let him know she was in fact pregnant.

This time around, he was going to take every precaution and immediately started the Heparin at a higher dose. There was part of me that still didn't find this safe and I feared that it would have some long-term effect on Traci or the baby. But the doctor assured us that this was the best technique and it was safe for both mother and baby so we went with it. We never told anyone about Traci's first two pregnancies because we always feared the unknown and this time was no different.

At the 10-week checkup the doctor was happy to report that everything looked good and she wouldn't need to be seen for another month. Initially we thought this was a long time, based upon the previous two pregnancies, but there was something about this time that felt different and the doctor seemed very happy with all the initial test results.

At 14 weeks we came back to the doctor to find out she was past the first trimester, when most of the problems occur. He even felt it was safe to tell friends and family that Traci was pregnant. This was a change for us because we weren't quite sure we wanted to just in case something happened again. Traci never wanted to hear people say "I'm so sorry.... you can keep trying." She knew that people just didn't know what to say in a situation like that so maybe it was best if we kept the news to ourselves until 20 weeks.

I was okay with this decision and in fact I was actually good with it because I was really nervous about becoming a dad. I had grown up with the greatest dad in the world, but what kind of dad was I going to be? I began to question everything, including our finances and housing situation, but Traci never wavered. She had confidence that we were ready and this time we were going to have a baby.

At 18 weeks we went in to find out the sex of the baby and while we were both hoping for a boy, for some reason we both knew it was going to be a girl. Most parents, especially in our situation, would just hope for a healthy child and while that's all we really cared about, there was no reason we couldn't disclose we wanted a boy. I guess I thought that if I had a boy I would at least be able to teach him sports and we would have this natural bond, just like my dad and I had when I grew up.

Within minutes of going to the appointment and getting the all-clear from the doctor, we were asked whether we wanted to know the sex of the baby. Of course we did! There was no way I could wait another 22 weeks to find out the sex of the baby. Some people are okay with painting a room neutral and then changing things after the baby is born. That is just not my M.O.

So there we were, Traci in the chair and the nurse giving her the ultrasound that would identify the sex of our baby. Within seconds the nurse said, "You are having a girl!" I will have to say, even though we had initially talked about wanting a boy, we were overjoyed to be having a little girl.

Still, our joy quickly turned to panic as the news made everything so much more real. Was I going to be able to handle a girl? Would I know what to do? My mind was going a mile a minute. As we left the office and discussed having a girl, Traci smiled and said, "Last night I had a dream it was a girl." She could see the fear in my face as I began questioning whether or not I would be a good dad. She comforted me a little when she reminded me of how little girls always love their dads and she was excited to see the bond the two of us would create.

Future doctor visits went incredibly well, and while Traci had only gained a few pounds, the doctors didn't seem to be worried. We were both nervous based on the past, but the tests showed there was nothing to be concerned about except low amniotic fluid. She was told the best medicine for this was bed rest for a couple weeks and they would check again.

At the next visit the levels had not gotten much better, but we were told not to worry. All of the measurements were coming back okay and the doctor was happy with her progress.

At 32 weeks Traci had finally gained a couple of pounds and the baby was growing. The doctors had told her the fluid had returned to a normal level. We were being told that she would have a small baby for some time now, but they didn't expect any complications during birth. That was great news to hear, but the doctor did want to increase the Heparin rate until the 38-week mark of the pregnancy. Traci was okay with this and she was told it would help with any possible complications.

We went to see the doctor at 36 weeks, only to be given crazy news. This was not our doctor but another doctor who said "It's almost time to say happy birthday to the baby." What? What the hell was he talking about? She still had four weeks to go and he made it sound like she was going to have the baby any time now. You can only imagine how I began to freak out about an early arrival of the baby and about fatherhood. I wasn't ready for this and wasn't sure if Traci was ready to be a mom. He said our doctor would be calling us in the next day or so but she needed to really take it easy until she heard from him.

The next day we did have a call of relief from our doctor who said she would be okay for another couple of weeks. I could breathe again. After another week we went back in and Traci was given a second stress test. The doctor checked the results and told us it would be good to schedule a day to check into the hospital because we were going to be having this baby a little early. He was not concerned about anything but said with the low fluid level it was best to induce her and have the baby early. Wow, that was a lot to comprehend as we went from relaxed to panic mode again.

On December 19, 2007, the hospital called at 1 am to let us know that they had a bed open and we should come to the hospital in the next hour and they would start inducing Traci. We had been told that the labor for a first pregnancy can take up to a day and a half and not to be surprised if we were there for a while. We have all seen the moms walking around the hospital in labor, trying to speed up the process. We brought quite a few movies with us and tried to make ourselves comfortable before she would start to feel the contractions from being induced.

By 9 am we were checked into our own hospital room and the contractions seemed mild, but Traci has always had a high pain tolerance, so it was very tough to tell. The nurse came in to check her and see how far she was dilated, and she was almost 7 cm. They hadn't given her an epidural yet and they didn't think she was going to be this far along yet. The anesthesiologist was also having a baby and the hospital was short one, so they were not sure if there would be time for her to get an epidural. I was starting to feel like I needed an epidural more than Traci or at least a heavy dose of Xanax, as my nerves were beginning to overtake me. Finally, at the last minute, Traci received an epidural. Everything seemed to be moving fast and before we knew it the doctor was in the room to deliver our 5-pound, 4-ounce beautiful girl.

We named her Petra Milan. T's family hailed from the Czech Republic and we wanted to use a traditional Czech name. The name Petra means "rock" and Milan is "our love." After so many disappointments in her previous pregnancies, we finally had our first child. She was very small but healthy and my heart was instantly hers the minute I saw her. We knew we probably would never be able to have another child and this little girl was going to be our rock.

Having a baby girl was so much different than I had ever expected. I was talking so much about having a boy that I didn't realize until she was born just how great it was to have a little girl. It seemed like she was the size of a football when she was born. We would swaddle her up into a tight little bundle that I would call a burrito and I would carry her around in my arms.

I had heard so many people tell me just how different life was going to be once I had a child. They warned that once she was born we could forget about our lives as we knew them because everything would be about baby. I never understood these statements. Sure, we would be spending a lot of time tending to our daughter, but I didn't think it meant our lives were over. To me they were the same as people who say once you settle down and get married, you can no longer have any fun in life.

The first few months of having a baby are quite different because you are still learning everything you never knew about caring for a little one. Friends had told us we would need plenty of toys and trinkets to keep the baby busy, but we decided that a few select items in the house would work. I've been to so many houses that are 100 percent dominated by play toys, covering any semblance of an adult living space. Yes, Petra was the most important thing to us in life, but it didn't mean that we needed to turn our house upside down and remove everything we had worked so hard to get. Our thought was that children don't need every toy in the world. We decided that spending quality time with her together was much more important than Petra having a house full of toys.

Family time has always been very important to me. It is one of the reasons I get up before the sun comes up on most days to complete my training runs. I want to be done before Petra and Traci get out of bed so I don't get to miss any time with them. It always makes me run a little faster during races, knowing that my family is waiting for me at the finish line. Traci and Petra have come to all of my races.

When you grow up with parents who run, there is no doubt you will eventually get the itch to give it a try. Petra is no different. She watches me run through the mountains and as I make my way into aid stations at races I often find her climbing up the rock formations or hiking on the trails. There is no question that she gets more excited about heading to the track than me. We often go as a family to time Traci, and she is out there running intervals with her mom. She knows the lingo and loves to be the "pacer" as her mom rounds the track. The pacer is basically a safety runner that keeps you alert during long races or focused in marathons. Petra is the only pacer I've ever come across that could make me smile no matter no badly I felt during a race.

Chapter 31: San Diego 100

In June of 2012 I set out to run my third hundred-mile event in a little over a year. I had two races in mind for the year and wasn't sure which one I wanted to do. For most people, one hundred-mile race in a year would be plenty, but my wife had faith in my ability. Since I couldn't decide which one I wanted to do, she suggested I sign up for both; so, acting in line with my lack of moderation, I decided again—why not? I registered for San Diego 100, which I would run in June, and then I registered to run Pine to Palm 100 in September.

Going into the San Diego 100, my mind was clear and focused. It wasn't until the race director, Scott Mills, began briefing the runners on the difficulty of the course that my nerves started to get the best of me. I also started to question how I was going to run Pine to Palm only three months after beating my body up on this course. Traci kept reminding me to not think about that race until it got here. I started looking at the topographic maps (not that I could really read one well), but the jagged lines indicating steep terrain scared me to death. My heart rate quickly escalated to a point where I thought it might explode. I felt more nervous than I had ever been before a race. I usually get race jitters at the start, but this was out of control. Sweat began dripping down my face and my palms were sweaty. Traci looked at me with an understanding that we should leave as soon as possible, so as to not make my anxiety attack worse. As soon as the briefing was over, I rushed to the hotel to take a Xanax.

Eventually I calmed down and managed to get my mind set for a good night of sleep. I would need it for the long day I was about to endure. Before I crawled into bed I got a couple of bottles ready by filling them with water and my race day drink. Traci and my sister Jill finished the bottles for me as I really needed to get some sleep and they would be crewing for me the next day.

Since the race didn't start until 7 am, I slept until 4:30. When I awoke, we quickly packed the day's supplies and left Alpine, Calif. to head for Al Bahr lodge in Mt. Laguna, where the race would start. It is about a 30-minute drive but since parking was tight, we figured it would be best to arrive around 6:15 to get a spot and make sure I had plenty of time to pace nervously around the start before the others arrived.

As with most ultras, the runners gathered a few minutes before the start, waited for final instructions and jumped around to ease their nerves. I've seen some listen to loud, fast-paced music to get themselves pumped up while others are quiet and seem to almost be meditating. I personally stand there with nervous energy, making idle conversation with others and trying to listen to the last-minute instructions although I can barely hear them over the nervous pounding of my heart in my chest. This day was no different and I clearly missed a few instructions, as I would discover during the race.

At the start of the race, I walked over to my wife and gave her a kiss. I looked for my sister and gave her a hug. Then we waited for the countdown. This was my sister Jill's first time crewing/pacing a trail race/ultra. She had run marathons before, which always have elaborate starts, so I briefed her ahead of time on how low-key the start of these races were. I wanted to make sure she didn't think people would be stretching, running strides and staring down their competition, waiting for the gun to go off or for the race director to say go.

We started promptly at 7 am and I slowly made my way out of the gate, trying to channel a smooth, easy pace. My friends had told me to start really slow and work my way up in the pack once my legs were fully stretched out. The only cool part of starting the race at the front of the line is you get to be in the picture on the website. But unless you know that you have the ability to finish top-three and a few extra feet at the start might mean the difference between first and second place, where you line up at the start is really irrelevant. These races aren't chip timed.

I only had one mantra for the day and that was to stay consistent and strong. I started in the front quarter of runners, knowing that most of the runners in front of me would eventually back off the throttle and I could make some adjustments once I got my breathing down. The first section of this course runs through the tall grass meadows and narrow trails, keeping participants from passing other runners. This was a blessing to me, because I didn't have to worry about being passed; I could just focus on my breathing. I was running at 6,000 feet of elevation and my breathing was slightly restricted for the first few miles, but I knew a nice smooth pace would take care of that. With about a mile before the aid station we had our first downhill. I had checked the course map out before the race and knew that this was the first of only two major downhills in the entire race. I have always excelled at the downhill portions so I flew down it like a bat out of hell. Several runners moved out of the way to avoid "the idiot in a yellow shirt" who was speeding down a very technical descent. I arrived at the aid station right on my projected time and quickly turned around and headed back out.

The mile 13.6 aid station is the last stop for crew access until mile 44 so I really needed to plan my game ahead of time to figure out how I was going to handle the next few sections. I was okay with liquids, carrying two hand-held bottles, but there was going to be a section later that concerned me so I asked Traci to have my hydration pack plus two hand-held bottles ready. I really didn't need or want to carry my pack that far but I just kept thinking about the course profile between miles 36 and 44 and I figured by that time in the day it would be hot. My pack was ready to go as I arrived at the aid station with an electrolyte drink, ice water, and an electrolyte gel shot mixed with 21 ounces of water for 400 calories.

The next few aid stations seemed to come and go rather quickly. I was making my way around this course well and was feeling great. Mile 31–36 is a lollypop-style loop. This meant the runners would pass an aid station and then after making a loop we would come back around to the same aid station before heading out to the rest of the course. This aid station was in the perfect spot, as it was just starting to get hot and they had ice buckets to dunk our hats in and volunteers who squeezed ice-cold sponges over our heads. I absolutely loved this because I was worried about overheating and needed this more than anything at the time. However, it did have some negative consequences. My clothes were now soaking wet so I started to worry about chafing.

As we made our way out of the aid station, the large black flies were relentless and my wet sweaty head had become a perfect target for them. My bald head was covered at all times with these annoying flies but unfortunately there was nothing I could do to avoid them, other than run faster to get out of this section.

About halfway through this loop, my friend Andrew from Phoenix caught up to me and we started talking about how the first part of the course had gone. We decided we should work together to make these miles go by a little quicker. The first three miles of this section are rolling but mostly uphill followed by some decent downhill before coming back into the aid station. With about a mile to go, he said he was starting to feel a little sick, and since we were moving at a pretty good pace, we backed off just a touch, hoping for revival at the aid station. He is not one who ever complains about anything, so to hear him say he wasn't feeling well, I knew the heat and humidity were getting to him.

We hit the aid station and saw our friends Michael and Jody heading out to start the same loop. Andrew again reiterated that he wasn't doing well. We cooled off with the ice buckets, downed some ginger ale and headed out up the dreaded asphalt road. I assumed this part of the course might last a quarter of a mile or so and then we would hit trail again, but instead it was three miles of ascent up the hot asphalt road.

If this was a normal road, we probably could have picked up our speed, but this road felt like a 20 percent grade in the exposed sun. Ugh! We hiked for a mile or so trying to keep each other's spirits up before Andrew told me to go ahead. He promised to catch up in a few minutes. I gave him a couple of Tums and then started to power hike as fast as I could to get to the top of the hill. At the top of the hill, there was a blessing from the race director. It was a makeshift aid station with ice water, bug spray, and another cold bucket to dunk our heads in. (Note to all race directors: this is a must-have on a hundred-mile course.)

I had started to pull away from Andrew a little at this point since his stomach wasn't cooperating, so I pushed on and ran the rolling hills until I hit the next helpful halfway aid station. I made sure to drink plenty of water and eat a popsicle that the volunteers were handing out. I wanted to cool down at this station because I knew the next portion of the trail included 2,500 feet of climbing. I credit the popsicle for boosting my spirits because I felt really good all through the next climb. I kept telling myself that I was going to get to see my wife and sister as soon as I made it to the aid station. It had been 5-1/2 hours since I had seen them and I was still right on my target pace.

Coming into mile 44 the head wind was crazy, but it didn't slow me down and as soon as I heard "Come on, Danek," I took off running as hard as I could. It is always a welcome sight to see family and I was greeted by family and friends at this aid station. It was only a brief visit before I gathered my thoughts and headed back out.

I really wanted to knock out the next section quickly so I could pick up a pacer at the next aid station. We climbed up the ridge and ran alongside the narrow mountain path that wound beautifully through the single-track trails for the next seven miles. Despite the head wind, this was a very runnable section of the race and the views of the trails and horizon below were breathtaking.

I picked up my sister Jill at mile 51.8 for her first-ever pacing duty and she was raring to go. I came into this aid station in 9.5 hours so I was well on pace to break 22 hours. I knew the last 49 miles of the race were more difficult but I would not have guessed they would be as hard as they were. Jill and I ran for a couple miles and everything felt really comfortable until we started to run the flat section through the tall grasses. I always prefer single-track running and even better if I'm surrounded by trees.

The trees prevent me from seeing the trail in front of me and I don't always like to see how far I have to go when I'm running, because it can be a mental drain. I was trying to take GUs (synthetic gel) for calories more often at this point but my stomach was just not cooperating. I slowed down to a walk for a few minutes and to complain. I really hoped to walk off the stomach issues. They are inevitable but did they have to hit me in a runnable section? We had to walk most of the way to the next aid station while I waited for my stomach to cooperate. Thankfully we were only passed by a couple of runners during this time. I wasn't worried because I planned to pass them again as soon as I could get going.

Jill ran with me until mile 64, where I picked up Traci for her first pacing duty of the day. She had been crewing all day, making sure I was eating, drinking, and moving along and now it was her turn to push me on the trail. We started off with some rolling hills in the woods, followed by a two-mile climb before hitting my favorite part of the course. It was pitch-black outside and all we could make out was the headlights from the runners around us. We had hit the top of the hill and caught up to a couple runners from San Antonio. They said we were welcome to go by but instead we decided to run together for the next six miles. While we had never met before we had some friends in common and we started telling stories that made the miles click off extremely quickly.

About 100 yards before mile 72 aid station, the wind picked up and I was really starting to feel the cold air. We could hear the generator at the aid station but right before it was a knee-deep creek that had to be crossed. The only way to the aid station was to cross the creek and the water was downright freezing. We hammered through the short creek and I made the executive decision to make a sock and shoe change. I have never done this in a race because it is tough to get compression socks off, especially when they are wet, but my next pacer. Vanessa Rodriguez, and her boyfriend Robert "Shacky" Shackelford helped me get them off and put some dry ones on.

I have always worn full-length compression socks that go up and over my calves since I started running, and these are to symbolize my dad and the medical-grade compression socks he wore after he suffered his first blood clot. I have worn them every day since I started running as a way to honor him. People have always asked me why I wear the socks and I say for recovery, but I couldn't tell you if they work. In my mind they were just another way for me to be close to my dad. While they're not always my favorite thing during the 115-degree days of summer in Arizona, my body does adjust to them and they have now become part of my look.

I had never met my next pacer before, but we had exchanged emails for a few days and we talked a little so I knew a little bit about Vanessa, but I didn't know what she would think of me after I had run 72 miles. I didn't want her to get a bad impression of me since I probably looked like hell and I like to jabber when I run. We had two sections to run together and they were going to be the most challenging sections of the day. The next 15 miles was almost all uphill and into the wind. We walked most of the areas and time flew by as we talked about trails, family, and ultra-running. With so many questions to ask a person I had never met, it made the miles go by fast and I hardly noticed the relentless climb. With a few miles to go, we started to talk about the Grand Canyon and she told me of her recent mountain lion encounter, and suddenly it hit me that it was her blog that I had read a day prior to going to the canyon to run Rim-to-Rim-to-Rim. After reading about a lion encounter, I was freaked out that I would run into one and not know what to do, but luckily there were no mountain lions that day.

Vanessa was great. She took me into mile 88 looking strong and really helped me from having any low moments. The rest of the race seemed to fly by. We were in and out of aid stations and before I knew it, Jill and I were skipping the mile 96 aid station and heading towards the finish line. She kept telling me that I had three miles to run and one mile to think about our dad and celebrate.

I always use that last mile of a race to solely think about my dad and, without fail, it brings tears to my eyes every time. As we made our way to the finish, Jill described the signs that I would see and then we saw the lodge. I naturally started yelling and hollering because my adventure was almost over. As we made our way close to the lodge we were told to head this way to the finish. We crossed through the flags and I made my way to the finish in 21:58:02. I was ecstatic, as I had made my goal by two minutes, but then I was told I was going to be disqualified for missing the bridge. My sister and I thought the volunteer who told us this was joking, so I said "Ha, funny." It wasn't a joke. They said we needed to go out and come back across the bridge in order for it to be an official finish. I had no idea what they were talking about, but we ran out, found the bridge and crossed it. When we finished this extra 0.1-mile circle and came back to the finish, the time read 22:01:26 and I had gone from 12th place to 13th. I wasn't happy at all, not because of the place but because I missed my time by a minute.

I learned a valuable lesson that day: it is not over until it is over. I really enjoyed the course, the unique flair of all the aid stations, and the swag was great at the race. This is not an easy hundred, if there is such a thing, but it was a fun hundred.

Chapter 32: End of the Streak

I knew I had been approaching the end of my streak. Day 923 was right around the corner, but I wasn't sure of the exact day it would land on. My website updates my run data each day and keeps track of my running streak, and as it neared 850, I realized it was just a matter of time before it was over. I had put so much thought into this streak and was reminded of it each morning when I awoke from sleep with burning calves, but I had never taken the time to figure out the last day.

By now all of my running friends and coach knew the rules of the streak and they accepted the fact that I would always run at least four miles every day, even if it was right after a race or a long run. Some of my friends thought I was nuts and they didn't want to run with me because they thought it was just a matter of time before I was injured and they didn't want to be the jinx.

There was a group of us who ran together several days a week, but mostly I ran with my friend Jeremy Dougherty. He was there for so many good and bad runs and it only seemed fitting that he would be the one to ask the question, "So when is the streak over? I know you're going 923 days and you're getting close, but have you figured out when?" I wasn't really sure and told him the start day of the streak and all during our run that morning we tried to figure out what the day would be. I figured it would be some day in early September and most of me was hoping it would land on the day when I would run the Pine to Palm 100 mile event. How great would it be to end the streak with the ultimate run? I figured it was too far off, though, since it wasn't until September 16th

We finished that run that morning and I went home and checked my website to see how many days into my streak I was so I could add up the number of days left and finally know which day was the last day. I thought it would be cool to start a backwards countdown in my house.

What I discovered was unreal. To me it seemed like a miracle and a sign from T. I added all the days up and when I looked at that calendar, the streak ended on September 23, 2012. This was the exact day T had passed four years prior. I went back in and checked my math again and it came out to the same day. I was completely blown away. I needed someone else to take a look and see if my math was correct; I have always been very good with numbers but this just seemed to be too good to be true.

I came running into the bedroom and woke Traci up and told her I needed to know if I was right that day 923 is on 9/23/2012. Traci knew the day was approaching but also had not taken the time to figure out when it would end. After a few moments waking up and thinking about it, Traci confirmed that the streak would end on 9/23.

I was blown away because when I started this streak I hadn't put one thought into the day it would end and I never once thought about it during the streak. There was a leap year in 2012 and I randomly started on the day we returned from a vacation from Italy.

I immediately grabbed my phone and called my mom, sister, and brother to tell them about the coincidence. They knew I had been running forever and they remarked about how great it was but again they had never looked at the dates to try to figure out when it would end. I think they thought I would probably break before the end of the streak, and that would have been okay, but when I passed the two-year mark they knew there was no stopping until I reached my goal of 923 straight days. My sister and her husband had both been part of my hundred-mile events, and my brother and mom were so instrumental in keeping me going that this felt like a day we could all celebrate as a family. This was not about me; this was about all of us and the perfect way for us to honor the man who made us who we are today.

Everything about this streak was emotional for me and this made it no different, but it made it very clear that there was no stopping until the end. As I said previously, I was hoping for the streak to end on the day of my Pine to Palm 100. This was even more fitting, but it would be just six days after my final hundred. This was both good and bad but, as anyone who has run 100 miles knows, the after-effects can be disastrous.

It hurts for days after you run a marathon, but it hurts really badly after you finish 100 miles. It is often difficult to walk, let alone run four miles. I was a little scared that I had mistakenly scheduled this race and should have figured out when the streak would end. After my first hundred-mile event my ankles were so large that it took two weeks for the swelling and pain to go away, and every morning I wasn't sure if I could run, but I had been able. What if I got sick? What if I ended up so dehydrated that I needed an IV? What if I was injured badly on the course and couldn't finish? Parts of me thought it might be best not to run in the race, to preserve my goal of finishing the streak, but mentally there was no way I was going to let that happen. This streak was about will power, strength, and persevering through difficult times, so why stop now? If something happened and I was hurt during the race, it obviously wasn't meant to be and I would just start over when I could run again, but I really never thought about anything except getting that shiny Pine to Palm 100 mile sub-24-hour belt buckle.

Chapter 33: Sodium-Enriched DNF

Just as my relationship with Traci took a different path than I had expected, so too did my journey along the Pine to Palm 100 race in Medford. We flew into Medford late Thursday night and when we woke up Friday morning, we started to drive around Ashland. This race turned out to be in one of the coolest little towns I have ever visited.

Having never been to Oregon, I wasn't sure what to expect, but what we found was a beautiful countryside with fall colors in full bloom and miles upon miles of wineries. If only I drank wine. Traci's eyes lit up when she saw all the vineyards, but not as much as when she saw famous ultra-runner Hal Koerner. Maybe it was his abs of steel, but I think it is his smile that most girls find impossible to look away from.

We picked up my pacer Van at the airport Friday morning. Since we had never met or even spoken before, we game planned a little for the race and got to know each other so the run Saturday would be more enjoyable for both of us. Van was relatively new to running ultras but had the passion, knowledge and talent that will make him a force in the ultra-scene for years to come.

After grabbing Van and race planning, we headed right over to Rogue Valley Runners running store to see if we could buy some of that magic potion that all of their employees must drink to make them elite ultra-runners. One of the first things you notice when walking under the purple-and-green sign is the trophy collection of store owner Hal Koerner. That is likely as close as I will ever get to the Western States 100 cougar. We picked up a few last-minute items and lots of stuff we didn't need; we love to support the trail-running community, so it was easy to spend money in the store.

I'm always a little nervous the day before a race, and that Friday evening was no different. The nerves went away quickly when we had the chance to meet ultra-running legends Scott Jurek and Hal Koerner at the pre-race meeting.

We hung around and talked for a little bit and then made the hour drive back to Medford to get some sleep before the big race. I took a few last long glances at the course profile and talked with Traci and Van about last-minute race plans. Then I was off to a medically induced sleep (with the help of Tylenol PM).

When we arrived at the race start, I stepped out of the car to try and shake the nerves, but walking around on a dark road out in the middle of nowhere did nothing for calming me down. About two minutes to 6, we walked towards the front of the pack to get a good starting spot for the race but what I found when I got up there was the race director, Hal, counting down from 10 to 1 to signify the start of the race. I ripped off my sweatshirt, threw it at Traci and we were off, heading up the five-mile climb to Rock Creek.

The first five miles of the race are straight uphill on an asphalt road but running this hill in the dark felt pretty easy. I ran with the lead group through this section until we hit the trail entrance, where I got lost. I know, big shocker that I got lost. There is usually an aid station at this spot to direct traffic but it was not needed Saturday because of the low temperature, and we just missed the turn. It was actually kind of nice because we got to head a quarter-mile back down the hill to gain momentum before we hit the trails. I was able to collect my breath from the climb and we took off through the leaf-covered forest. The first hour of the race was a little dark, but no headlight was needed, in my opinion. Nevertheless I carried that damn light on my wrist for the first 42 miles of the race.

Running through the deep fallen leaves was great, and even though I couldn't look up to see the surroundings, I loved what we were running through.

The first nine miles of uphill seemed to fly by rather quickly, and I knew once we got to that point it was straight downhill to the mile 15 aid station. My body was in good shape at this point but I decided it was best to hike the final little climb and let a couple people go by me before I took off down the hill. It was at this point that a famed female ultra-runner passed me and I started to run with her the rest of the way up the hill. When we got to the peak, I assumed I would pass her on the way down, but what I found was she was an amazing downhill runner and she took off flying down the hill. We weaved in and out of rock croppings, through puddles and eventually out of the forest to the mile 15 aid station. This was one of my best sections of the race and it was good to have someone to talk to while we ran down the slopes at a fast pace.

About 0.1 miles before the aid station I took a glance at my watch. Big mistake. I lost balance and found my face buried in dirt, eating leaves off the ground. I brushed myself off with no damage and jogged into the aid station, smiling about my misfortune.

Just past mile 15, the trail turns into forest roads. I am not a fan of running on forest roads, but I did find them helpful in this race because it allowed runners to make up lost time due to the amount of climbing on the course. We ran a pretty quick pace from mile 15 to mile 22 where we were greeted by the Scott Jurek aid station, which seemed to give all the runners an extra boost. It is always nice to hear how good you look from a guy who has won the coveted Western States 100 trophy seven times in a row.

I started to hear some rumblings after mile 22 from other runners about the forest roads, but again we were all on cruise control, so I figured why stress over something that will save you time. It wasn't like we were just finding out that there were quite a few miles of forest roads, so I wasn't sure why so many were complaining about them.

Mile 28 was the location of the first crew stop and also the Seattle Bar aid station. This is known as the Hal Appreciation Station. All of the volunteers were dressed in full Hal Koerner gear: fake abs, beards, and the patented Rogue Valley Runners hat tilted to the side. I cooled off in the ice bucket, grabbed an energy drink and some chips and headed out. The problem was that I exchanged bottles with Traci just seconds before and I had mistakenly left my energy gels tied to the bottle I left with her back at the aid station. There wasn't much I could do about it, but I was worried as the next five miles included a pretty steep climb that would surely suck the energy from me.

It seemed that this race had one brutal climb after the other, but I managed to hike them pretty fast. The sun had come out at this point and it was starting to get warm. It was not warm by Arizona standards but being 30-plus miles into a race, the little bit of sun that was hitting me felt like a furnace blast. The heat slowly began taking its toll on me and slowing down my pace a little but no one seemed to be passing me, so I figured they must have been suffering more than I was.

After four or five miles of climbing I hit another long downhill and all of a sudden I had the life back in my legs. It was there that I made up time I had lost on the climb and I really felt like I was moving as I made my way into the Squaw Lake aid station. Squaw Lake has a two-mile loop around the lake before you see your crew again and head up the road towards Squaw Peak. The first half of the loop felt great and I was running around a nine-minute-mile pace on the flat ground, but the second mile I started to feel a little cramping in my legs and was slowed to 14-minute pace while I walk/ran to the aid station. It wasn't bad but just enough to be annoying, so I took down some potato chips and fruit and headed out.

I wasn't one mile into the next section before I started to feel the cramps again, but this time they were more intense. I stopped momentarily to drink some extra electrolyte drinks to ensure I was properly hydrated. Stopping only seemed to aggravate the problem. I complained a little and started running again, but within a half mile I was brought to my knees by the intense cramping in my calves and hips. I had softball-sized bulges appearing in my calves and I was immobile for a few minutes. Most cramps are caused by dehydration, but I didn't feel dehydrated. I was drinking plenty of fluids and carrying three bottles, so I was pretty confused by my condition. After sitting for a few minutes, I had a few runners pass me and I finally asked one for some salt tablets. I bit into the tablets and poured the salt in my mouth in hopes of alleviating the problem.

Momentarily I felt better, but it wasn't 100 yards later that I was bent over the side of the trail throwing up. I wasn't quite sure what had made me sick but now I was feeling dizzy, dehydrated from throwing up, and slow. I took a couple more salt tablets to try and balance out all the water I was drinking, but as has happened to me so many times, I overdid it with the sodium. Instead of waiting for the sodium to get into my system and help with the cramps, I looked for an immediate solution and I failed. I threw up on and off all the way into mile 50 and the pain in my stomach was getting worse by the minute.

The mile 50 aid station is just a brief stop where runners make a one-mile climb to get a flag at the top of the peak and head back down to give it to the aid volunteers. I had arrived at mile 50 in 10:18 and left mile 52 in 12:30: I took just over two hours to make a one-mile climb up and a one-mile run down. I couldn't walk, couldn't run and during this stretch, more than 20 runners passed me. I lay down in the middle of the road. After a while I crawled to the side, trying to hide in some tall weeds. I didn't want the other runners to notice how sick I was. I was puking non-stop. Runner after runner kept asking if I wanted help.

Trying to remain confident about my ability to finish, I gathered myself and prepared for the next 50 miles. I was ahead of schedule, had already run 50 miles and climbed 15,000 feet so I knew there would be no more than 7,000 feet of climb left over the last 50 miles. When I finally composed myself and left the aid station, I headed out behind the second-place female, who had suffered the same fate about eight miles back. She now also appeared to be rebounding. I was hoping to stay with her but right out of the aid station she ran hard up a long eight-mile climb, chasing after the female leader. This section was all gravel roads and while I was getting tired of seeing gravel, I sure did find it comforting to lie on.

Cars were passing me, kicking dust up, and every time one was coming, I would stand up long enough to let them go by so I would not be medically pulled from the race. I was still throwing up, wasn't able to keep anything down and at this point my body was on empty. I faced another problem that I had not anticipated, and that was darkness coming before I got to mile 65. It had never crossed my mind that I wouldn't reach this point by 8:15 pm, especially after getting to mile 50 at 4:18 pm. It took me almost four hours to get through this stretch of the race. I carried that damn headlight on my wrist for the first 42 miles and then left it with Traci at one of the aid stations—only to finally need it.

I was struggling at mile 60 but my spirits were raised when I saw my friend Chuck and he gave me his headlight to get up to mile 65. I slogged the next five miles up the hill and finally reached Dutchman aid station in 15 hours. As I came up the dark slope I could hear Green Day's "Wake Me up When September Ends" blaring at the aid station and I was feeling better about my position. I had 19 hours to finish the next 35 miles—pretty easy, huh? The music pumped me up and I got excited about finishing the last 35 miles of the race.

As I approached the lights in the distance, my mood lightened as I moved to the song lyrics. At that moment it felt like this song was going to save the day, but the lyrics rang in my head. I couldn't wait for September to end, let alone this race. I sat for a minute and put on some warm clothes. Again, I got sick to my stomach and puked more fluid than I thought was capable of coming out of my body. Traci and Van tried to get me up and moving but I was dizzy. They tried to get me to drink soup broth but it tasted horrible. Ginger ale tasted worse and my body was cramping terribly. Volunteers were squeezing the bulging cramps in my legs as I sat in the chair, until finally I decided I needed to keep moving.

Traci was going to join me for another one-mile uphill to get a flag at the top of Dutchman Peak and then one mile down back to the aid station. We made it no more than 300 yards and I was on my knees projectile vomiting again. What was wrong with me? I told Traci I was done, and she could go ahead and get out of the cold and walk back to the aid station. After she made her way back down the hill, I gathered myself and started to make the long climb up the hill, sitting every tenth of a mile to try to calm my stomach. It was no good; it took me 40 minutes to climb to the peak. When I got to the top, I looked back to see Traci right there, saying I had left her at the bottom. I said I needed to keep trying and wasn't ready to quit yet, but the downhill did me in. I couldn't walk without cramping or throwing up but thought if I made it back to the aid station, I could take down a few calories and finish the race. As I sat, the pain was so intense and I was so sick that I finally asked the volunteers to cut off my P2P bracelet.

I was done, my first ever DNF (Did Not Finish), and while I knew the disappointment would ultimately consume me, I had made the right decision. I might still be out there crawling if I hadn't pulled myself from the race. What started off as such a great day ended in sodium-drenched failure.

Chapter 34: Nearing the End of an Era

While I couldn't find my way to the finish line of the Pine to Palm 100, I was nearing the end of my 923-day streak. The race took place on September 17 and I had just six more days of running left before the streak would be over.

I knew when I went to bed that night after the race that I still needed to run four miles into Sunday. I also knew I would be hurting and probably still sick when I awoke, but I was going to have to get out there and complete the mileage anyway. I would need to complete it before we hopped on a plane back to Phoenix.

When I awoke that Sunday morning, my body was revolting and my calves felt like someone had beaten me with a baseball bat the night before. I could barely walk and wasn't quite sure how I was going to pull off four miles. To make it worse, our hotel was quite a ways from any trail; I was going to have to run it on the pavement. My legs don't seem to respond very well to the pounding of the pavement and while I knew I would run faster on the roads, it didn't really matter because I could barely bend over to put my socks on my legs.

That morning I decided that I wanted to run by myself because I knew I was going to be bummed out from the night before. It was the first time that I had ever had to drop out of a race and that feeling had kept me up all night long. I wasn't sure exactly how to deal with my first "Did Not Finish" label but I thought some alone time would allow me to work through the anger. When I replayed the previous day in my head, I knew I had made the right decision. I was truly in bad shape and would have spent a significant amount of time getting IV fluids the next day if I had attempted to keep going. Ultimately this might have cost me my streak with just six days to go, so I was content with my decision-making. Naturally it is common to be upset when you don't finish something you have worked very hard for, but from the beginning, running hundred-mile races had nothing to do with my goal of running 923 straight days of four miles. It was for my dad.

I ran those four miles as though they were my first day running during the streak. The pain seemed to be masked by the fact that I was about to accomplish my goal. I suddenly felt like a huge weight had been lifted from my shoulders and I was in the home stretch. I had thoughts of running 10 to 20 miles during this run but there was a plane heading to Phoenix that I had to be on.

During those 35 minutes of running, I learned a lot about myself and I remembered exactly how I had gotten to this place to begin with. Through hard work. I never once worried about my pace, how far I was going, or what place I was in. I only cared about finishing what I had started three years before.

Sometimes failure is the best way to motivate a person, and this was no different. I had just a handful of days left to run and crazy emotions were starting to take over my mind. My schedule for the next week was just four miles every day. This would get me to the final day on Sunday, when I would host a run to raise funds for the National Blood Clot Alliance in my dad's name and celebrate with my friends and family.

When people started to hear about the run, my inbox was flooded with emails from friends and even strangers asking if they could be part of the run too. I was honored that so many people, including some I had never even met, wanted to be part of this special event.

As I drove around town completing last-minute orders before the big weekend, I received an email from my friend Sandra Stathis. She has been a big supporter of my writing for a long time and when she saw the streak was coming to an end, she reached out to a friend with a brief description of what I had been doing:

> Jay Danek's is a very moving and inspiring story about transforming grief and loss into a force for good. Jay was 100 pounds overweight and not physically fit when he suddenly and unexpectedly lost his father to a pulmonary embolism three years ago. After six months of grieving, he took to the McDowell Mountains, at the encouragement of his wife, to find some solace and to start moving forward. It took several months before Jay could run four miles. By then, he had become hooked to the peace he experienced on the mountaintop. The 20–30 seconds he

> spent each day at the summit, reflecting on the good times with his dad, kept him going… The rest is truly extraordinary. In the past four years, Jay has gone on to become an elite runner, competing in 100 mile races. He placed ninth, and set a personal PR, at last fall's Javelina Jundred. As Jay quoted in his blog… "Success isn't how far you go, but the distance you traveled from where you started." He is a father, husband, businessman, active member of the community and a warm and humble man. This Sunday he and his family will host a fundraiser and celebration run to benefit Stop the Clot and the National Blood Clot Alliance.

Shortly after the email arrived in my inbox another quickly appeared.

> Good afternoon, Jay, this is Connie Sexton with the Arizona Republic newspaper. I received an email from a friend of yours named Sandra and I wanted to see if we could do an interview for the Sunday paper? Your story has captured the hearts of many and I would like to see if we could talk this afternoon. If you're interested please let me know.

***

I was honored that someone would make such an effort to help get my story out about my dad and why the National Blood Clot Alliance means so much to me and my family. (Thank you again Sandra and Connie, what an incredible tribute for my dad by allowing me to talk about his life.) I received news that I would be interviewed for the Sunday paper and was absolutely floored and moved in a way I cannot describe. It was so moving to me that I was going to get to share my story about my dad and why the National Blood Clot Alliance means so much to me and my family. After hearing this news, I went to go meet Traci and Petra at AJ's, our local grocery store. We go there several times a day to get our iced tea so I didn't think anything was out of the ordinary when Traci told me to meet her there. We were sitting down for a moment and as I was telling her about the interview, someone walked up and put their hands over my eyes from behind me. This day had already been a whirlwind and my heart just about skipped a beat when this happened, because I was caught so off-guard. When I turned around it was my mom and sister, who had surprised me by coming out from Michigan to celebrate the last day of my running streak.

I have to say I had absolutely no idea they were coming out and usually no surprise ever gets past me. Remember, I was the kid that opened all his Christmas gifts ahead of time and learned to rewrap them perfectly so I wouldn't ever get caught. This surprise was by far the best part of my day, or year for that matter. It is definitely fun to be interviewed for the Sunday paper but to have family celebrate this milestone with me was huge. This was not just a day for me; it was a day for my mom, who was married to my dad for 36 years before he passed, a day for my sister to remember and reflect on memories of T, and a day for my brother Bryan to do the same.

Since the initial shock of his passing, my family had wanted to celebrate T's life in a big way for some time and now this was the perfect way to do it. While I still was unsure about how the last day was going to go, I was now clear that this was going to be a day that none of us would ever forget.

As I laid my head down on my pillow the night of 9/22/2012, one day before the end of my streak, a flood of different emotions came over me. I was anxious, depressed, nervous, excited, sad, fearful and also happy. I knew that the next morning I was going to accomplish my goal of running 923 straight days to honor T who died on 9/23/2008. I tried to picture how the next morning was going to go. I wondered if I would tear up when it was time for me to stand before my friends and family and give a speech about how lucky I was to have them all there and how special this day was for me. I wanted to celebrate this day the way I knew T would have wanted me to. I also thought about the day after my streak was over. What was I going to do when I woke up Monday morning and the running streak that had kept me going for so many days was over? Would I feel the need to run or would I be content taking a break on day 924? Since the streak had become such a big part of my life, I wondered what life would be like without it. I wondered if I'd be the same person.

Chapter 35: Celebration Run for T

Day 923 of the streak started very early for me. For the 923rd day of my streak to actually land on 9/23 without me planning it that way felt like a sign. I've never been one to check horoscopes or really believe in "signs," but this was clearly meant to be. I awoke from a dead sleep at 1 am. So many times during the streak, I would just go run if I woke up in the middle of the night because what else does one do when they can't sleep?

I was anxious and ready to go. I thought about heading out the door early and completing four miles on my own so I could be alone when the emotions of the day came pouring over me. Again, my impatience was starting to get to me, but I had 70-plus people showing up in the McDowell Mountains at 6:30 am to celebrate those four miles with me. I fought the urge to run early, went back to sleep for a few hours and eventually headed to the mountain around 6 am. While I didn't get any sleep that night, I felt completely rested and ready for an incredible day to start.

Since I arrived at the trail head early, I was able to see car after car roll into the Gateway parking lot. The number of friends who had come to support me was amazing. People even drove two hours up from Tucson to be part of the festivities. Because I always wore yellow when racing, I had yellow technical T-shirts made for anyone who was coming to run with me. They had McDowell Mountain Man in bold letters across the chest. This is the term that had been used to describe me as my journey started in the McDowell Mountains. We actually ran out of shirts that day because so many people came to run.

As the clock clicked closer to 6:30 am, the trailhead filled with people wearing bright yellow shirts and the level of excitement I felt was beyond my wildest expectations. Since this wasn't a race, I truly expected to see about 10 to 15 people show up, but when I had heard that 70 people were coming and then saw that many or more arrive I was completely shocked and overwhelmed with emotions. It seemed that somehow my story had touched people. There were people I have known for a few years and others who had just read my blog and wanted to be part of it.

It was so great to meet so many new people from the running world and to also run with friends and family. I know no matter what I write about T, I could never do complete justice for the kind of dad he was to me, but to see 70 people show up who had never met my dad before was unreal. One by one, people came up to me and my mom and told us that they could see just why he was so special and what an amazing thing we were doing to celebrate his time.

We had two different runs set up: one was the 4.3-mile Gateway Loop where my running career started 30 months prior, and the other would be the seven-mile Bell Pass out and back. The plan was to send one group clockwise and as we made our way back down Bell Pass and merged with the Gateway trail, I would pass the four-mile mark and we would all run in together to celebrate my dad's life and the end of the streak.

I chose to run the seven-mile route for one selfish reason. I wanted that run to last much longer than four miles. When I ran my first hundred miles and was in extreme pain at mile 99, it all went away during the last mile where it felt like my dad carried me to the finish line. I wanted that feeling for at least three miles and that was exactly what I had.

After ascending Bell Pass and getting the opportunity to run a little with everyone that came out for the day, I wanted to make the descent into the four-mile mark something I would remember forever. I knew there was only one other person that was going to be brave enough to run at full speed with me down the steep rocky slope, so Jeremy Dougherty and I gave the group a little start and then took off and ran that downhill faster than I have ever gone before (borderline reckless). We were both under control heading down in a sub-four-minute-a-mile pace. I'm pretty sure that is the first time I've ever seen my watch read a sub-4:00 pace.

As we got close to the four-mile mark, I wondered if I would burst out in tears. With my heart beating and emotions running high, I crossed the four-mile mark and felt an overwhelming sense of joy. To my surprise I didn't cry, I just smiled and took in the moment. I was with my friends and family and it was a day of celebration, not mourning. T would say that we had mourned enough and it was time that we remember the past but also time to move forward.

Before I laced up my running shoes, I was headed down a path of self-destruction. I was not prepared for T's death. No one can prepare for such a thing. It consumed me and I felt I could not control my life. To have a goal or ambition seemed hopeless without him around to be proud of me for the outcome. I could have easily given up after my father's passing, chosen to shut down, and to not take advantage of all that life has to offer. I almost did. But, with a little push from my wife to hit the McDowell Mountain trails I found a reason to really live again… and I found T.

I speak to him every day atop the mountain or towards the end of a hard training run. I know he is proud, looking down on me. Even if I never ran another day in my life, I know he would still be proud of me. Sometimes all I need is a headlamp, a mountain and a moment with T.

I started running because it saved me. I continue running because I've "got to live."

Chapter 36: Writing is My Therapy

I have always found writing and talking to my dad to be the best forms of therapy, and with just two days until my final run, I thought I would write my dad a letter to explain just what he meant to me. I knew he was smiling down on me at all times but I wanted him to know why I've been smiling and pointing up at the sky to him for so long.

Be Still My Friend (September 21, 2012)

Dad,

Sometimes talking to you while I run is just not enough, so there is no better way for me to express myself than through my writing.

First, I can't begin to tell you how hard it is every day to wake up and know that I will not ever get to talk to you in person again. I love to talk to you while I run, but what I wouldn't pay to see you for just a few minutes or talk to you again. I have come a long way over the last four years since losing you, but it never seems to get easier. Everyone always says that time heals all wounds, but it never changes the outcome. I wake up daily wishing life was like a game in that you only have to sit down momentarily until the next game starts.

When I hear Petra say "I miss Papa," or "When can we see Papa again?" it breaks my heart. That little girl was only 8 ½ months old when she lost you, but damn if she doesn't remember her time with you. She looks up at the pictures of us in Hawaii and while she might not remember definite details, it is clear that you were instantly a presence in her life.

Petra loved every minute of that trip to Maui with you and Mom. Maybe it was the talk you two had after the luau or maybe she remembers you stealing her kiddies' tent on the beach, but it is clear she remembers you. She talks to you while we ride in the car together and some days when I can feel your presence, she tells me things about you as if you were sitting right next to her. That little girl loved her Papa; even though her time with you was way too short, she will never forget.

I have to thank you for the gift of helping me find Traci. Do you remember that May afternoon when we went to the casino and you talked about how great of a girl Traci was and I told you she was a lot like you? She is a patient, loving, kind person who has a passion for life that I just didn't have at the time when we met. The two T's, as you guys used to call yourselves, seem to know every one of my moves before they even happen. You two know my tendencies, weaknesses, strengths, and most of all you two know exactly what keeps this guy balanced. People often say that men marry someone like their mom but in this case I married someone like my dad. I found someone with your patience, perseverance, strength, and someone that never overreacts even during my worst moments. This girl is special, just like you told me the first time you met her. I just wish I had listened to you sooner.

I have tried to be strong lately and grow a little bit as a person each day, but I still miss the life lessons that you taught me along the way. I have never tried to describe to my friends why you meant so much to me, because I don't think anyone would really understand just what you and Mom did for us kids to make us the people we are today. When I was a teenager I would have understood if you threw your hands up and tried to separate yourself from my rebellious nature, but you didn't, and for that I am forever thankful. Too many parents in the world don't really understand what it takes to be a parent. It is not about trying to be the cool parent; it is about shaping a kid's life. It would be easy to be that kind of parent but it is not easy to be the parent who loves their child more than anything and is willing to give up everything to make sure they are an upstanding person. All teenagers have issues and I was not alone, but not all teenagers move past their issues and that may be because they didn't have someone strong like you to guide them and see them through good and bad times. Yes, you could have walked away, but that was never in your nature. It was never about you; it was always about the family.

It has been a tough four years with you gone, but we all try to take one step at a time. We keep taking steps forward and trying to get through each day just as I know you are. I know you're with your dad and sister up in heaven, and I can only imagine when your sister joined you way too early in her life, "Sissy's Song" by Alan Jackson had to be playing in your head, because it has been playing in ours ever since that day.

As I approach the end of my running streak, I thought I would share some things with you that I learned along the way. I know you never were a runner and neither was I until four years ago, but running is how I rallied. Running helped me stay balanced and move some of my negative energy to positive energy. So what exactly have I learned by running 923 straight days?

1. Patience. I'm not like you but I have learned to accept that things take time. Since I wasn't ever a runner I had to learn to be one, starting with the day I went out and ran a tenth of a mile and was excited about my progress. I was 100 pounds overweight and I just ran one-tenth mile; it was my starting line and 9,400 miles was my finish line.
2. Passion. It had been so long since I felt passion for something outside of my family. I love to get out there and challenge myself by attempting feats I never thought were possible. I didn't even know what a hundred-mile run was until three years ago. When I heard about these races I thought they were asinine, and now I'm the crazy one out there running in them.
3. Pride. The people around me have filled me with so much hope, and every day when I cross that four-mile mark and my watch beeps, I look up at the sky and I think of how proud you would be. You wouldn't be proud because I ran four miles; you'd be proud that I set out to do something and never let anything stand in my way.
4. Family. What does family have to do with running? Everything. The running community has become my family. Traci and Petra have provided so much support for what I do that I can't help but be elated every time I look at them and think it is because of you that I have them today. These two attend every running event I have

and there is no question that seeing them during a race gives me that extra motivation to continue on.

Running has taught me to be alive again and live my life the way you always wanted me to. You never taught us to hold back, but to unleash our passion and presence on something we wanted and to go for it. I have been asked why I run ultra-marathons and not marathons and simply put, I love the long moments in time that I have with you every time I step out on to the trails.

You taught us to never waste a moment of life, and when I hear the song "Any Minute Now" by Colin Hay, it reminds me of you telling me to get everything I ever wanted out of life before it is too late.

I could go on and on about what I have learned through running, but we have our whole lives to talk about that. Every time I set foot on the trail and you see me look up and I smile, you know I'm thinking about you. This streak has been a whirlwind for me and some of the craziest things have happened over the last 30 months. Can you believe that on a whim I said I was going to run 923 straight days and the last day happened to land on 9/23? How does that happen? One could say dumb luck, but I think it is just fate.

I know you were always a numbers guy just like me and that's why my streak has so many ridiculous categories to it, but I know you love to see how all the pieces fit together to make up the puzzle.

Here are some fun stats that I know you would find interesting. You and Traci have always been two people that loved to enrich your mind with what I would call useless knowledge, so here are some fun facts for you two on the streak:

1. On Sunday I will have run 923 straight days with a minimum of four miles per day. Some days I wonder "What the hell was I thinking," but I only need to look up to remember.
2. 9,400 miles run and 19 pairs of shoes. The people at Inov-8 will be happy with me, since 14 pairs were their X-Talon 212s and 3 pairs are the 195s. That is the equivalent of

running from my house in Arizona to your house in Michigan and back 2.5 times. I bet you remember how long that car ride was for you and me when I first moved back to Michigan from Arizona, but can you imagine running it 2.5 times?

3. I lost close to 100 pounds and burned over 1,100,000 calories. That is 314 pounds of fat burned during the streak. Since I only lost 100, I guess I overate quite a bit.
4. 975,000 feet of elevation gain. I climbed the equivalent of Mt. Everest 75 times and I'm still here to talk about it. You're probably laughing at that one, thinking about me complaining about having to walk all the way up that huge hill in Jerome. I haven't been back since we went, but that must have been a 20,000 foot climb; okay, maybe 40 feet.
5. I ran 22 ultra-marathons (any distance over a marathon) and finished 21 of them. As you know, I failed to finish Pine to Palm 100 last week but I gave it everything I had, and unfortunately I was too sick to get past mile 67. I ran four 100-mile events, finishing three; two 100K's; five 50-milers; and 11 50K's. Sometimes I raced to see where I stood, but mostly I raced because it is a way for me to have hours to think about life.
6. I ran in Arizona, Michigan, Ohio, California, Oregon, Utah, Massachusetts, Texas, Hawaii, Nevada, and South Dakota. I can't forget that outside of the US I had the chance to run in Italy and Mexico. I wish I could keep track of all the cities, but I would bet it's in the hundreds.

It's pretty crazy to think about it being over this Sunday morning but, as I have said, Monday I will rest. On Tuesday I really don't know what I'll do but it is doubtful that my feet will not hit the trails at some point. I think I could just keep running but who really cares how many days one runs in a row. I didn't run all these days because I wanted the praise; I did it because I wanted to have to have another special bond between us.

I want to leave you with some funny things that have happened while you've been gone.

1. We have almost taught Mom to use an ATM machine, but she still likes to go inside the bank and hand-write checks. We'll keep working on this with her.
2. Petra has officially surpassed my knowledge of the Spanish language at the age of four. I embarrass her if I try to speak the language, so I'm only allowed to speak English.
3. I've learned that yelling at the TV isn't really my direct line into the Michigan Stadium to change the play call. Apparently they don't care what I think. I'm not fully on board with this one yet.
4. McDonald's cup holders still only come in brown, but all cars have four or five of them built in them. (On a family trip, when T was asked if he would like a cup holder for his drinks, he responded with "What colors do you have?" While I wasn't there I still laugh, picturing the drive-thru clerk's face saying "Uhh, brown?" For those of you who remember when cars had basically no cup holders and people used to hang those classy plastic holders from their windows, apparently T wanted one to match the car's interior.)
5. Jill now has her own credit card for all the purchases at The Gap. I know you told her a girl has to live, but it must feel good to not wonder what you didn't buy at The Gap this month.
6. Bryan now has three kids and is grooming another top-notch baseball player, with Colin playing ball with 11- and 12-year-olds. I saw him last week and met Mason, and luckily Bryan never asked me to play golf. I can't say I miss the golf aspect of you guys coming out every summer, but I do miss the fun we used to have. Bryan and I were discussing the infamous wine/tequila party last

week; pretty amazing that everyone survived that evening.

7. I started my own website and really have gotten into writing after work over the last couple years. I hope to write a book someday, but first I need to build some type of following. My site is called McDowell Mountain Man, named after the mountains I run daily and where I feel most comfortable. While I will always be an average runner, I think there is some hope for me to write some good stories later on in life. The website is a fun activity and takes my mind off the stresses going on, and maybe someday I will develop a little following and get a few more pages in the novel done. This will never be a money-maker, but it sure is fun.
8. I still can't read a map and get lost almost everywhere I go, but I love the adventure.
9. While you and I have always hated Notre Dame, it still brings a tear to my eye every time I see Rudy make the tackle at the end of the game, and think back to all the tears running down your face at the end of the movie no matter how many times you watched it.
10. Finally, I think Traci has taken over for this family where you left off and I see so much of you in her every day and, as you know, I would never make it a day without her. She knows what makes me anxious or upset just like you did and she makes me smile hundreds of times a day.

On Sunday we have over 70 people coming to the house to celebrate the life of a man most have only read about. How cool is that? That is why I also call my friends family.

We've had so many good memories and there are so many more memories to come. We know you're here with us in spirit every day and are looking down, helping make sure we make good decisions and live up to our potential in life. While the streak will end in a couple days, I will never stop thinking about you every time I run, walk, hike, or wake. I miss you and know you're proud of us all. Keep smiling and making us smile.

Love you T,
Jay

Chapter 37: To Those Who Supported Me

To everyone that supported me along this crazy venture and kept me motivated to go out and run each day, thank you. To Traci, who always made sure, no matter where we traveled, what our work schedules were, and even passed up on so many of her runs just so I could get four miles in, I owe you.

I took September 24th, 2012 off. For the first time in over 30 months I did not run one single step. I could easily have mustered four miles, but the day was not about me. The streak was way bigger than any individual. For me, it was about family, life, motivation, and the honor of celebrating the man who took such great care of us for as long as he was with us. People asked me if it felt weird not getting up and running. Honestly, I felt content with my decision. Anyone can run 923 days straight if they put their mind to it, but not everyone can walk away. I know I did the right thing and while I was back out running on day two after the end of the streak, it still felt incredible to know that I made it through such an incredible journey. I'm not giving up racing or running, but I'm going to slow it down a little, make more time for my family and live in the moment, because that is the most important thing to me.

As I sit here writing what will be the final pages of my story, I think it is important to leave you, the reader, with a few things.

Nothing in life is unattainable. No one can tell you what you can and cannot accomplish.

Grieving is hard but necessary. In order for you to properly grieve for a loved one, you must find your own inner calling or strength. I had no idea my calling would be running or spending time in the mountains, but that is where I am able to find peace with my dad's passing and where I can talk to him still today.

***

The final lesson...

Life is tough—very tough. No matter what challenges find you, you can overcome them. We were all given the power to deal with tragedy and to help others in their time of need. It is up to us to figure out how to use this power.

When asked if I have any regret for taking the day after my streak and celebration of my dad off, I answer with absolutely not. I have run every single day since that day (now at 207 and counting…), but this could all end tomorrow. I have no plans for any new streak; I just love to run. In November I had the chance to be a mentor at the Team Red, White & Blue trail-running camp in Texas. The men and women in this camp taught me so much about life and motivation. In the future, when times get tough and I want to quit running or quit at any challenge life will throw me, I will remember the men and women of Team Red, White & Blue. They battle every day through war injuries and every day they overcome. I received a Team RWB bracelet and an eagle shirt while I was at camp. These are small daily reminders of strength, honor and courage, and I feel stronger just being a part of this team. While my current streak doesn't align with anything regarding Team RWB, I am proud to be part of the eagle and as long as this is on my wrist I'm not sure I will ever stop, just as they never stop fighting for us.

Acknowledgement

This book could not have been possible without the love and support of my wife Traci and daughter Petra. You two are my rock, and when I have fallen, you have helped me back up. It's your smiling faces that get me out of bed each morning and push to be a better dad and husband. You have made the last 12 years an amazing adventure. We were always meant to be together and I can't imagine a day without you two. I love you two more every day.

To my brother Bryan Danek and sister Jill Conte. Thank you for all of your support and inspiration over the years. I have you to thank for so many of the great blessings in my life, as you helped guide me down the right path and see the wonderful things that are right in front of me. There is no way I could have completed this book without Jill's time and willingness to see me succeed. Love you both.

Special thanks to family friend Kristi Fitzgerald for the countless hours of reviewing my book and helping me bring my story to life. She has been instrumental in bringing my thoughts and feelings out in the book. She put her personal time and commitments aside and saw me through on this project from the beginning to the end.

To Tere Zacher who has been there since my first ultra-marathon. You have been an amazing friend helping me pursue my dreams of running and writing. Without a push from you there is no way I would have toed the line at the Night Run in pursuit of 46.2 miles. With your help I not only finished the Night Run, I finished three 100-mile races and 22 ultra-marathons.

Last but definitely not least, I need to thank John Vaupel and Jeremy Dougherty. These are two people that believed in the streak and were there from the beginning to the end. When I stopped believing in writing a book, John built me the website www.mcdowellmountainman.com which allowed me to put all my thoughts down in print, and it pushed me to continue writing. When the streak was in jeopardy, it was Jeremy and John who pushed me across the four-mile mark every day and they never let up, including running with me the last four miles on day 923.

About the Author

Jay Danek holds a Bachelor's Degree from Michigan State University in Crop and Soil Sciences. He currently works as the General Manager of West Coast Turf. Jay writes and publishes articles for mcdowellmountainman.com and trailrunningclub.com.

21831764R00136

Made in the USA
San Bernardino, CA
08 June 2015